LITTLE BOOK OF
CROONERS

WRITTEN BY
David Curnock

LITTLE BOOK OF

CROONERS

First published in the UK in 2007

© Demand Media Limited 2014

www.demand-media.co.uk

Printed and bound in Europe

ISBN 978-1-910270-11-0

CONTENTS

FRED**ASTAIRE** 4–7

FRANKIE**AVALON** 8–11

CHARLES**AZNAVOUR** 12–15

TONY**BENNETT** 16–19

PAT**BOONE** 20–23

AL**BOWLLY** 24–27

MICHAEL**BUBLÉ** 28–31

NAT**KINGCOLE** 32–35

PERRY**COMO** 36–39

HARRY**CONNICKJR** 40–43

BING**CROSBY** 44–47

VIC**DAMONE** 48–51

BOBBY**DARIN** 52–55

SAMMY**DAVISJR** 56–59

SACHA**DISTEL** 60–63

EDDIE**FISHER** 64–67

ENGELBERT**HUMPERDINCK** 68–71

JULIO**IGLESIAS** 72–75

JACK**JONES** 76–79

FRANKIE**LAINE** 80–83

BARRY**MANILOW** 84–87

DEAN**MARTIN** 88–91

AL**MARTINO** 92–95

JOHNNY**MATHIS** 96–99

MATT**MONROE** 100–103

JOHNNY**RAY** 104–107

JIM**REEVES** 108–111

FRANK**SINATRA** 112–115

RUDY**VALLEE** 116–119

SCOTT**WALKER** 120–123

ANDY**WILLIAMS** 124–127

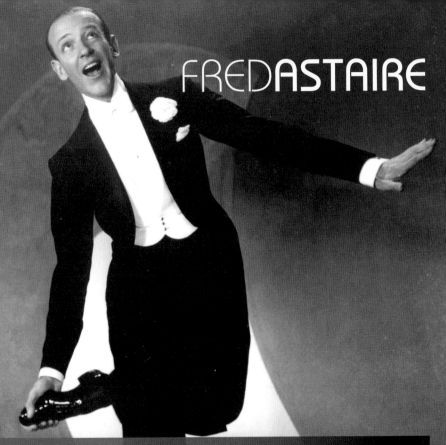

FRED**ASTAIRE**

Birth name: Frederick Austerlitz
Born: May 10 1899, Omaha, Nebraska
Died: June 22 1987
Years active: 1905 – 1981
Record label(s): RCA Victor, Brunswick, Columbia, Decca, Mercury, Verve, Kapp Records, United Artists

Perhaps best known as a song and dance man, as the result of his vaudeville background and a series of screen musicals starring alongside Ginger Rogers, the elegant Fred Astaire was a respected crooner in his own right. Although he often claimed he could not sing, he introduced some classic hits from The Great American Songbook that have stood the test of time. Without achieving the volume of record sales as some, he nevertheless brought great songs to the fore with his distinctive vocalisation of hits such as, "Night and Day" and "Cheek to Cheek."

Fred Astaire was born Frederick Austerlitz in Omaha, Nebraska, on May 10 1899. His father, Frederic Austerlitz, was an immigrant from Austria who worked as a salesman for the Storz Brewing Company. Fred's father played the piano and was fascinated with the world of show business, as was his mother, Johanna. The daughter of the family, Adele Marie, was almost two years older than Fred and, when she was six, enrolled in a dancing academy. In 1905, the family moved to New York after a temperance movement had caused the brewery to shut down. The family, soon to adopt the surname Astaire that was believed to come from an uncle, duly enrolled Adele in a dancing school with an eye to her future career prospects. Fred soon joined her as part of a dance act that went on to make its professional debut in Keyport, New Jersey, in November 1905 when Adele was eight years old, and young Fred was six.

With varying degrees of success, their vaudeville career continued, eventually making it onto Broadway in 1917 with Over The Top. Fred had already made acquaintance with George Gershwin, who was working as a song plugger. More shows followed and, with increasing acclaim, they rose to the top of the bill. A flop show in 1923 saw them move to England to appear in the West End in *Top Flirting*, and also record their first UK only release, for HMV, with two songs from the show. On returning to New York, they starred in the Gershwin smash hit *Lady Be Good* that ran for 330 performances, followed by another 336 when they brought it to London. Back in the US, another hit show, *Funny Face* was also brought to the UK in 1928, where it repeated its success.

In 1932, Adele gave up her career to marry Charles Cavendish, son of the Duke of Devonshire. Fred continued his stage and recording career as a solo act, recording "Night And Day" in 1933. He was soon given a screen test that, in spite of being criticised for his looks, led to a film contract with RKO. This led to a legendary cinematic pairing with Ginger Rogers in 10 musicals. Astaire recorded many of the hit songs from the films,

LITTLE BOOK OF CROONERS

among these were, "Cheek to Cheek," "No Strings," "Isn't This a Lovely Day?" "Top Hat, White Tie and Tails," and "The Piccolino." By the end of the 30s the films were losing money so the partnership with Ginger was ended. Fred made films for several studios, and continued recording, before signing a long-term deal with MGM. His 1946 recording of "Puttin' on the Ritz" from the hit film *Blue Skies*, reached No 2 in the *Billboard* charts.

At the age of 47, Fred decided to give up dancing to concentrate on owning and breeding horses. Gene Kelly broke his ankle just before filming was due to start on *Easter Parade* so Astaire was asked to deputise. His retirement had lasted less than a year, and Fred continued working on films, radio and television. The 1958 one-hour special *An Evening with Fred Astaire* won him nine Emmy awards. Serious film acting, notably his performance in *On The Beach*, and his role in the musical *Finian's Rainbow* took care of the 1960s, with more film and television work keeping him busy into his 70s. In 1975 he made three LPs in England for United Artists, and the following year saw Fred making more films and television movies, earning him his third Emmy Award for Outstanding Actor in a Special.

At the age of 78, Fred broke his wrist while playing around on his grandson's skateboard; this event brought him lifelong membership of the National Skateboard Society. Twice married, the first in 1933 to the Boston socialite Phyllis Potter with whom he had two children, Fred Jr, born in 1936, and Ava, born in 1942. Phyllis died from cancer in 1955, when Fred was making the film *Daddy Long Legs*. His second marriage, in 1980, was to Robyn Smith, an actress turned jockey, almost 45 years his junior. On his death from pneumonia, in 1987, it was revealed that one of Fred's last requests was to thank his fans for their support.

FRANKIE AVALON

Birth name: Francis Thomas Avallone
Born: September 18, 1940, Philadelphia, Pennsylvania
Years active: 1951 - present
Record label(s): Chacellor, RCA Victor

Frankie Avalon is considered one of the first manufactured teen idols. He started out playing backup trumpet in a local band called Rocco and the Saints, and it was there that local impresario Bob Marcucci discovered the future teen star.

Eight months later, Frankie's first single, "Cupid," came out on Marcucci's Chancellor label, and his third release, "Dede Dinah," hit the Top 10. Frankie had his first No. 1 single in 1959 with "Venus," and went on to release six more Top 40 records in that year alone. Marcucci nudged Frankie away from rock, following the successful run he was having with easy-listening crooning fare.

Indeed, Frankie enjoyed 31 charted US Billboard chart singles from 1958 to late 1962, including "Just Ask Your Heart", "I'll Wait For You", "Bobby Sox to Stockings" and "A Boy Without a Girl" He was less popular in the UK but did still manage four chart hits with "Why", "Gingerbread", "Venus" and "Don't Throw Away All Those Teardrops".

Although the singer's four-year domination of the music charts was coming to an end, his career wasn't. He teamed up with Annette Funicello and reinvented himself as a clean-cut, pretty-boy surfer in the wildly successful Beach Party surfer film series.

Frankie also had straight dramatic parts in the John Wayne historical western film The Alamo, as well as the science-fiction story Voyage to the Bottom of the Sea with Barbara Eden.

A symbol of his era, Frankie appeared in the 1950s-themed musical Grease in 1978, playing The Teen Angel and singing the memorable "Beauty School Drop-out" in the film. "Kids know me from their Grease DVD, so they instantly respond," he would later say. "You can hear a pin drop when I do my old songs."

In 1985, Frankie embarked on a 50-city tour with Fabiano "Fabian" Forte and Bobby Rydell known as "The Golden Boys of Bandstand," which was broadcast by PBS as a segment of On Stage at Wolf Trap in 1986.

The following year, the still-youthful-looking Avalon reteamed with Funicello for the light-hearted throwback Back to the Beach (1987), which included a notable performance of the song "Pipeline" by Stevie Ray Vaughan. He made a cameo appearance as himself with Robert De Niro in the 1995 film, Casino.

Frankie married former beauty queen Kathryn "Kay" Diebel on January 19, 1963 after meeting her while playing cards at a friend's house. His agent warned Frankie that marriage would spoil his teen idol mystique. Still together, they have eight children and 10 grandchildren.

LITTLE BOOK OF CROONERS

Frankie has used his youthful appeal to create Frankie Avalon Products, a line of health and cosmetic aids, which he promotes on the Home Shopping Network.

In recent years, Frankie has starred in stage productions of Grease in the role of Teen Angel and in Tony n' Tina's Wedding as a caricature of himself. Additionally, in 2007, he performed "Beauty School Dropout" with the four female contenders for the role of Sandy on the NBC television reality show Grease: You're the One that I Want!

In April 2009, Frankie appeared as a guest on the hit television show American Idol, where he sang "Venus." One of his more unusual claims to fame is a mention in The Vaccines song 'Teenage Icon' where they sing they are no teenage icon, "no Frankie Avalon".

CHARLES
AZNAVOUR

Birth name: Shahnour Varinag Aznavourian

Born: May 22 1924, Saint-Germain-des-Prés, Paris

Years active: 1933 - present

Record label(s): EMI, Barclay, Mercury, Monument, Ducretet Thomson, MGM, Polydor, Reprise, MusArm Records

Charles Aznavour may be small but he stands tall as one of France's most popular and enduring singers. Known for his idiosyncratic tenor voice, clear and ringing in its upper reaches with gravelly and profound low notes, he has appeared in more than 60 movies, composed more than 800 songs and sold well over 100 million records.

In 1998, Charles was named Entertainer of the Century by CNN and users of Time Online from around the globe. He was recognized as the century's outstanding performer, with nearly 18% of the total vote, ousting Elvis Presley and Bob Dylan.

Described as "France's Frank Sinatra", Charles sings frequently about love in multiple languages including French, English, Italian, Spanish, German, Russian, Armenian, Portuguese and Neapolitan.

He is best remembered in the UK for his song "She" which went to Number One in the charts in 1974 and was followed by "Dance in the Old Fashioned Way".

Artists who have recorded his songs and collaborated with Charles include Édith Piaf, Fred Astaire, Frank Sinatra (Charles was one of the rare European singers invited to duet with him) Andrea Bocelli, Bing Crosby, Ray Charles, Bob Dylan (he named Charles among the greatest live performers he's ever seen), Liza Minnelli, Elton John, Petula Clark, Tom Jones, Shirley Bassey, José Carreras, Nana Mouskouri and Julio Iglesias.

A tireless tourer, Charles performed in London for the first time in 25 years at the Royal Albert Hall in October 2013; demand was so high that a second concert at the Royal Albert Hall was scheduled for June 2014 by which time he will be over 90!

The reviewer for The Daily Telegraph, Neil McCormick, commented: " The fantastic quality of Aznavour's songs and the sheer charisma of his presence hold the centre. His audience proved as devoted as teens at a One Direction concert. When he threw a cloth into the front rows at the end of La Bohème, there was an unbecoming scrum, with a bearded white-haired gent scrabbling on the floor in a tug of war with a bountiful woman in a red dress. Further proof, perhaps, that music keeps you young. "

He has had a long and varied parallel career as an actor, appearing in more than 60 films. Short and stubby and excessively brash and brooding, he was hardly leading man material but embraced his shortcomings nevertheless. Unwilling to let these failings deter him, he made a strong impression with the comedy Une Gosse Sensass (1957) and with Paris Music Hall (1957) which kickstarted his movie career. One of his most notable roles was in The Tin Drum, winner of the Academy Award for Best Foreign Language Film in 1980.

LITTLE BOOK OF CROONERS

With Armenian immigrant parents, Charles helped the country through his charity, Charles for Armenia, following its catastrophic 1988 earthquake. Together with his brother in-law Georges Garvarentz he wrote the fund-raising song "Pour toi Arménie", which topped the charts for 18 weeks. There is a square named after him in central Yerevan and a statue erected in Gyumri, which saw the most lives lost in the earthquake.

Charles has been married three times - to Micheline Rugel (1946) Evelyn Plessis (1956) and Ulla Thorsell (1968) – and has six children: Séda, Charles, Patrick, Katia, Mischa and Nicholas.

Standing just 5 ft 3 in tall, he has neither stunning film star looks nor a particularly remarkable voice, but he has two things in his favour - powerful on-stage charisma and incredible willpower. For a man who once said, " My shortcomings are my voice, my height, my gestures, my lack of culture and education, my frankness and my lack of personality, " he hasn't done badly!

TONY
BENNETT

Birth name: Anthony Dominick Benedetto
Born: August 3 1926, Queens, New York
Years active: 1936 – present
Record label(s): Columbia, MGM Records, Improv (Bennett's own label)

O ften referred to as The Singer's Singer, Tony Bennett has many admirers. In a 1965 interview for Life magazine, Frank Sinatra said, "For my money, Tony Bennett is the best singer in the business. He excites me when I watch him. He moves me. He's the singer who gets across what the composer has in mind, and probably a little more."

Anthony Dominick Benedetto was born, and grew up, in the Astoria neighbourhood of Queens, in New York City. His father, a grocer, died when Tony was 10 years old, leaving his seamstress mother to support her family. The youngster spent much of his spare time drawing pictures in chalk, on the sidewalks around his home. At the age of 10, his vocal talent was highlighted when he sang at the opening ceremony of the Triborough Bridge in 1936. By his teens, he was already set on a career as a professional singer. After briefly studying art, he left to help support the family, working as a singing waiter in Italian restaurants. Drafted into the US Army at 18, Bennett served as an infantryman on the front line in France and Germany, and later sang with an army band, using the name Joe Bari.

After the war, Bennett studied singing, learning the Italian *bel canto* voice discipline, while still working as a waiter. His interest in jazz led him to vocally mimic the phrasing of jazz musicians. His improvisational ability earned him a place in singer Pearl Bailey's 1949 show, in Greenwich Village, to which Bob Hope had been invited. Hope invited Bennett to join his touring show, but advised him to drop the name Bari. In 1950, Bennett made a demonstration disc, and was duly signed for Columbia Records. His first big hit, "Because of You," sold over a million copies, and was in the charts for 10 weeks, reaching the No 1 position in 1951.

His 1952 marriage to Patricia Beech dismayed his female fans; around 2,000 of them, wearing mourning black, had gathered outside St Patrick's Cathedral, New York, for the ceremony. The couple had two sons, D'Andrea (known as Danny) and Daegal, shortened to Dae, both of whom would become important influences in Bennett's later career. A third No 1 hit, "Rags to Riches," topped the charts for eight weeks in 1953. International fame was achieved when his record "Stranger in Paradise," from the show *Kismet*, reached No 1 in both America and Britain. Even during the downturn that coincided with the rock era in the late 1950s, Tony was able to achieve eight *Billboard* Top 40 entries.

When pianist Ralph Sharon became his musical director in 1957, Bennett made a highly acclaimed, jazz-orientated LP, *Beat of My Heart*. Collaboration with Count Basie

LITTLE BOOK OF CROONERS

led to two more successful albums, *Basie Swings, Bennett Sings,* in 1958, and *In Person!* which featured the song "Chicago," in 1959. His reputation soared, culminating in a sold-out concert at Carnegie Hall in 1962. That year he recorded his signature song, the double *Grammy*-winning, "I Left My Heart in San Francisco." It stayed in various charts for a year but, surprisingly, only made No 19 in the *Billboard* Hot 100. Apart from another Top 5 album, his parting company with Ralph Sharon in 1965 coupled with the rise of Beatlemania sent Tony's career into decline.

Divorced in 1971, Tony married Sandra Grant in 1972 with whom he had two daughters, Joanna and Antonia. His recording label, Improv, had some success with two albums and the single "What Is This Thing Called Love?" before failing in 1977. By 1979, he had no recording contract and, in 1980, was divorced. Drug addiction took hold and, in desperation, he called his sons for help. Danny, a good businessman, became his manager and moved him back to New York, to sing in smaller venues. Re-united with Ralph Sharon, he signed for Columbia in 1986 and reached the charts with his album *The Art of Excellence.* Gradually, his career recovered; his albums *Astoria: Portrait of the Artist* (1990), the Sinatra tribute *Perfectly Frank* (1992), and his Astaire collection *Steppin' Out* (1993), with the latter two going gold and winning *Grammys,* firmly placed the artist back at the top. In 1995, his *MTV Unplugged* was *Grammy* Album of the Year.

Inducted into the Big Band and Jazz Hall of Fame in 1997, Tony has a star on the Hollywood Walk of Fame. Still touring, Tony has made some of his most memorable albums in recent years.

In August 2006, at the age of 80, Bennett made his album Duets: An American Classic, followed five years later by Duets II, on which he sings with such legends as Aretha Franklin, Willie Nelson, Lady Gaga and British soul singer Amy Winehouse. Their song Body and Soul was reportedly the last recording she made before her tragically early death from a drugs overdose in July 2011.

LEFT
Tony Bennett performing on stage with Jazz drummer Art Blakey.

BELOW
Tony Bennett singing at the Royal Command Performance, 1965.

PAT**BOONE**

Birth name: Charles Eugene Patrick Boone
Born: June 1 1934, Jacksonville, Florida
Years active: 1954 – 2000s
Record label(s): Republic Records, Dot, London, Rediffusion (in the UK), Hip-O Records, The Gold Label

A singer who came to the fore during the 1950s, Pat Boone has crossed over several musical boundaries. From popular ballads, R&B, country and gospel, he has blended chameleon-like against different musical backgrounds, as well as standing out in front of others. His, at times, outspoken political and racial views seem at odds with his religious upbringing and family background.

Charles Eugene Patrick Boone, better known as Pat Boone, was born in Jacksonville, Florida, on June 1 1934. He is, reportedly, a direct descendant of the famous American pioneer, Daniel Boone. When he was two years old, his family moved to Nashville, Tennessee, where he spent his childhood. Pat attended David Lipscomb College, a Church of Christ sponsored private high school, now a university, in Nashville. He started singing, professionally, while a student at North Texas State College in Denton, Texas. In 1953, while only 19, he married Shirley Lee Foley, daughter of country music star Red Foley. The Boones, who have remained married ever since, are parents to four daughters, Cherry, Lindy, Debby, and Laury. His daughter Debby has followed a career in music, and had the *Grammy* winning, top-selling US single in 1977 with "You Light Up My Life."

Recording for Republic Records from 1954, he had a massive hit with a cover of "Ain't That a Shame," outselling the Fats Domino original. Remaining in the R&B cover business for the early years of his recording career, Boone made the music of many black performers more acceptable to the white population during the civil rights problems in the US at that period. Although he made six hit R&B covers, including that of Fats Domino, only four were rock songs including "Tutti Frutti" and "Long Tall Sally," previously hits for Little Richard. The two blues ballads, "I Almost Lost My Mind" and, "Chains of Love," the latter a hit for both Big Joe Turner and BB King, set Pat Boone straight down the middle-of-the-road, musically. Following in the footsteps of his idol, Bing Crosby, he scored several massive hits with ballads such as, "Love Letters in the Sand," "April Love," "Friendly Persuasion" and "Don't Forbid Me."

Boone became something of a style icon to the American teenagers, with his clean-cut, wholesome appearance and trademark white buckskin shoes, and was second only to Elvis Presley in popularity. He appeared in several films, most notably *April Love* in 1957, *Journey to the Center of the Earth* (1960), and *State Fair* (1962) in which he made his only on-screen kiss. He also wrote the theme music for the film *Exodus*. Pat also hosted a networked television series late in the 50s. His last Top 40 hit, in 1962, was the novelty record "Speedy Gonzales." As musical tastes changed, Pat moved toward the country music and gospel sections in the

LITTLE BOOK OF CROONERS

record stores, as well as performing in radio. He and his family also took to the road to tour with a gospel show in the 1960s and 70s.

It has been well documented that Boone is a devout Christian, brought up and partly educated in the Church of Christ. His moral standards were often at odds with the demands of show business, causing him to decline work that he believed would compromise his religious beliefs. Born-again, Pat has been a member of the Pentecostal church for over 30 years. With their home in Los Angeles, Pat and Shirley still attend church regularly.

A previous neighbour of the Boones was the rock singer, Ozzy Osbourne, formerly lead singer with Black Sabbath. Pat made a cover version of Osbourne's hit song "Crazy Train" that became the theme song for *The Osbournes,* a reality documentary TV series. Ozzy reportedly said that Boone had never complained about living next door to his unconventional family.

In recent times, Pat has become a disc jockey on radio, and runs his own record label that specialises in new recordings by former great artists from the past who no longer interest the major labels. His company, The Gold Label - Honest Entertainment, releases records made by singers of the calibre of Jack Jones, Glen Campbell, Patty Page, Cleo Laine, The Four Freshmen, and Roger Williams, as well as the proprietor himself. In 1997, Pat released an album of heavy metal covers that he performed in his own style, *Metal Mood: No More Mr Nice Guy.* His achievements in gospel music were recognised in 2003, when he was inducted into the Gospel Music Hall of Fame.

In August 2006, he wrote an article for the online periodical *WorldNetDaily* in support of actor Mel Gibson, who had allegedly made anti-Semitic remarks. Unlike many singers immersed in the world of rock 'n roll, Pat has been married for more than 60 years, with four daughters and 15 grandchildren, and has lived in the same Beverly Hills house for nearly 50 years. His right wing Christian beliefs have courted controversy, but his views have been voiced with sincerity and enthusiasm and have not damaged his legacy of one of America's legendary crooners.

LEFT
Pat Boone in rehearsal for the Royal Variety Show in 1958.

BELOW
A close-up of Pat Boone, 1960.

AL BOWLLY

Birth name: Albert Allick Bowlly

Born: January 7 1898 (or 1899), Lourenco Marques, Portuguese East Africa (now Maputo, Mozambique)

Died: April 17 1941, London, England

Years active: Mid 1920s - 1941

Record label(s): Broadcast Twelve, Brunswick (in USA), HMV (in UK), Columbia, Decca, Durium, Edison Bell

A l Bowlly might be a surprise choice in a book celebrating the best crooners of all time but he deserves his place in history as the inventor of crooning.

Born on January 7 in 1898, Albert Allick Bowlly was a Mozambican born South African who became a popular jazz crooner during the British dance band era of the 1930s. He recorded more than 1000 records between 1927 and 1941 with his most popular including "Midnight, the Stars and You", "Goodnight, Sweetheart", "The Very Thought of You", "Guilty" and "Love Is the Sweetest Thing".

He made his first record in Berlin in 1927 where he recorded Irving Berlin's "Blue Skies" with Edgar Adeler, and one year later arrived in London for the first time as part of Fred Elizalde's orchestra. That year, "If I Had You" became one of the first popular songs by an English jazz band to become well known in America. Despite this transatlantic success, the onset of the Great Depression in 1929 resulted in Al being made redundant and resorting to several months of busking to survive.

In December 1931, Al married Constance Freda Roberts in St Martin's District, London but discovered his new wife in bed with another man on their wedding night! The couple separated after a fortnight and were granted a rapid divorce. He remarried in December 1934, this time to Marjie Fairless, the marriage lasting until his death.

During the mid-1930s, songs such as "Blue Moon", "Easy to Love", "I've Got You Under My Skin" and "My Melancholy Baby" were sizeable American successes—so much so that Al gained his own radio series on NBC and travelled to Hollywood to co-star in 1936 with Bing Crosby, one of his biggest competitors, in The Big Broadcast.

He had appeared with his own band, the Radio City Rhythm Makers, but they had split by late 1937 when his vocal problems were traced to a wart in his throat, which briefly caused him to lose his voice. Once again down on his luck, he was forced to borrow money from friends for a trip to New York for much-needed surgery in 1938.

His absence from the United Kingdom damaged his popularity with British audiences. His career also began to suffer as a result of problems with his voice from around 1936, which affected the frequency of his recordings. Al moved back to London with his wife Marjie in January 1937, but never really explained why he had returned with rumours that he got mixed up with a gangster's moll.

With his diminished success in Britain, he toured regional theatres and recorded as often as possible to make a living and underwent a revival from 1940, as part of a double

LITTLE BOOK OF CROONERS

act with Jimmy Messene (whose career had also suffered a recent downturn), with an act called Radio Stars with Two Guitars, performing on the London stage. The partnership was an uneasy one, as Messene suffered from a serious drink problem , and was known to turn up incapable on stage, or to not turn up at all, much to Al's consternation. His last recorded song, made two weeks before his death, was a duet with Messene of Irving Berlin's satirical song about Hitler, "When That Man is Dead and Gone".

On 17 April 1941, Al and Messene had just given a performance at the Rex Cinema in Oxford Street, High Wycombe. Both were offered the opportunity of an overnight stay in the town but Al opted to take the last train home to his flat at 32 Duke Street, Duke's Court, St James, London. His decision proved to be fatal, as he was killed by a Luftwaffe parachute mine that detonated outside his flat later that evening. Although the massive explosion had not disfigured him, it had blown his bedroom door off its hinges and the impact against his head proved fatal. He was buried with other bombing victims in a mass grave at the Hanwell Cemetery where his name is given as Albert Alex Al.

Al remains one of the most highly regarded singers of his era because of his extraordinary range, his command of pitch and rhythm, and, above all, the sincerity with which he could deliver a lyric. Noble is often quoted as saying that Al often stepped away from the microphone with tears in his eyes; "never mind him making you cry, he could make himself cry!"

LEFT
Big band singer and guitarist Al Bowlly

BELOW
Al Bowlly

MICHAEL BUBLÉ

Birth name: Michael Steven Bublé

Born: September 9 1975, Burnaby, Vancouver, Canada

Years active: 1988 – present

Record label(s): 143 Records/Reprise Records, Warner Elektra Atlantic (Italy)

I t was my Grandfather Mitch who is still my best friend who introduced me to this kind of music. He would play a record of Sinatra, Dean Martin, Ella Fitzgerald, Bing Crosby or the Mills Brothers on an old record player. I never saw these singers on stage, I only listened to their music but everything I was going to learn I pretty much learned by listening to the lifetime's work of these artists." So said Michael, recalling his early musical memories.

The eldest of three children, Michael Steven Bublé was born in a suburb of Vancouver BC, Canada, on September 9 1975. He has two sisters, Brandee and Crystal. Michael is very proud of his Italian family origins; he is particularly proud of his Italian grandfather, Demetrio Santagata, known as Mitch, who captured young Michael's interest in the jazz and ballad singers from the golden years of song. By the age of five the Bing Crosby hit, "White Christmas" was being sung by the youngster, many times over and often out of season, around the house. Michael's singing talent was obvious from the age of 13, when he entered, and won, a local talent contest. However, he was disqualified for being underage; he was compensated four years later, when he won first prize at the nationwide Canadian Youth Talent Search.

In his teens, and while still at high school, Bublé sang in hotels and clubs in the evenings and at weekends, and occasionally helped out on his father's salmon fishing boat. In order to obtain the club and hotel bookings, his grandfather Mitch, a plumber, offered to carry out plumbing work at the venues in return for the proprietors allowing his protégé to perform. When he was 17, Michael took lessons from voice coaches. He was soon offered work on the Red Rock Diner Roadshow that was organised by a Vancouver 'retro' radio station, and toured throughout the US; part of his act was an impression of Elvis Presley. His future girlfriend, Debbie Timuss, also appeared on the show although it has been claimed that they first met while both were in a musical review, *Forever Swing*.

In 1996, Michael recorded the first of three independent albums, *First Dance*, which was made for his grandfather, and not released. In the next three years or so, the Bublé career was marking time, with him recording demo discs, appearing in minor television shows, and singing at a series of small gigs that failed to swell his bank balance by any large degree. He had considered the prospect of leaving show business entirely, as he could see no way forward. His second independent album was *Babalu,* recorded in 2001, but not a great commercial success. However, its first track, "Spiderman Theme," was re-mixed and used as the theme tune for the film. His third independent album, in 2002, was entitled *Dream*.

LITTLE BOOK OF CROONERS

LITTLE BOOK OF CROONERS

In September 2000, Michael was singing at a corporate engagement where he met a person who, unknown to him at the time, was to have a profound impact on his future career. Michael gave the man one of his CDs and told him that, if he did not like it, it could be used as a beer mat. The following day, the man called him on the phone and told Michael that he was an aide to no less a person than Brian Mulroney, the former Prime Minister of Canada. He asked Bublé to perform at the wedding celebrations after the marriage of Mulroney's daughter, Caroline. The aide also told him that David Foster, the head of the American label 143 Records would be attending and would like Michael to sing for him. This resulted in the signing of a recording contract with Foster's company, a subsidiary of Atlantic Records. Early in 2001, Bublé went to Los Angeles to start work on his first major-label album that would be released through Reprise Records.

The album Michael Bublé reportedly took nine months to make, and was not released until February 2003. Featuring a range of standards including "Fever," "Sway," "Come Fly With Me" and "That's All," the album was an instant success. Within a year, it had sold over 2 million copies world-wide, over half a million in the UK alone, and went double platinum in Australia. The chart-topping albums have continued to flow: It's Time (2005) Call Me Irresponsible (2007) Crazy Love (2009) Christmas (2011) and To Be Loved (2013) were all number ones. Happily married to actress Luisana Lopilato and with a young son, he continues to tour around the world with his 2014 tour starting in Finland and ending in Mexico taking in Manchester, Glasgow and Birmingham along the way.

NAT
KINGCOLE

Birth name: Nathaniel Adams Coles
Born: March 17 1919, Montgomery, Alabama
Died: February 15 1965, Santa Monica, California
Years active: Mid 1930s to 1964
Record label(s): Capitol

O fficial US census records show that Nathaniel Adams Coles was born in Montgomery, Alabama on St Patrick's Day 1919, although he claimed on various documents to have been born in 1915, 1916, 1917 and 1919. The eldest child of Edward James Coles and Perlina Adams Coles, he was brought up in the Bronzeville district of Chicago. His family was understandably very religious, partly due to his father's calling as a pastor, and the fact that his mother was the daughter of a Baptist minister. Although his father was against popular music, Nat's mother, herself a capable organist, encouraged him to play the piano from an early age. He took formal lessons from the age of 12, and his repertoire expanded to cover not only jazz and gospel music, but also the classical works of Bach and Rachmaninoff.

In his teens, Perlina persuaded Edward to allow their son to play jazz, in return for him providing the music at the pastor's Sunday services. His passion for jazz led him to hanging around outside clubs where artists such as Louis Armstrong and his particular idol, Earl 'Fatha' Hines, played. Nat soon began performing, with his older brother Eddie Coles playing the bass, in their own band in jazz clubs where he acquired his appellation, 'King', presumably from the Old King Cole rhyme; somewhere along the way he dropped the 's' from his surname.

The band made their first recording in 1936, under Eddie's name. The next step on Nat's career ladder was as pianist on a touring revue *Shuffle Along*, but this show failed while on the road in Long Beach, California, where Nat decided to remain. His career moved away from his jazz roots around the early 1940s and, although he was accused of selling out, his move into mainstream popular music was to prove a very successful, and profitable, transition. His first popular hit was a recording of the self-penned "Straighten Up and Fly Right," based on a folk story used in a sermon by his father. The record was released by Capitol and sold over 500,000 copies, thus beginning a long association with that label.

Another of his greatest mainstream offerings was "The Christmas Song," which he recorded three times: first in 1946, then in 1953 when he incorrectly sang "reindeers", and again in 1961, probably the most-played version. With a string of hits in the late 1940s and early 1950s, including "Nature Boy," "Mona Lisa," "Too Young," and the aptly-named "Unforgettable" that became his signature tune, it was claimed that Nat's success financed the building of Capitol Records' distinctive circular headquarters building at

LITTLE BOOK OF CROONERS

Vine Street, Los Angeles. Known to many as 'The House that Nat Built', it was the first building of its type in the US, when constructed in 1956.

In 1948, Nat bought a house in the hitherto all-white Hancock Park district of Los Angeles. The local property owners association made it clear to Cole that they did not want any undesirables moving in, to which Cole reportedly replied, "Neither do I. And if I see anybody undesirable coming in here, I'll be the first to complain." In this period in America the problem of racial difference was ongoing; on one occasion Nat was attacked, in a possible kidnap attempt, while on stage in Birmingham, Alabama, leading to his decision to never appear in the Deep South again. It also sparked his political activities. His networked television programme *The Nat King Cole Show*, in December 1957, the first TV show to be hosted by an African-American, closed down due to the reluctance by national companies to invest their sponsorship. Nat claimed that, "Madison Avenue is afraid of the dark." Having previously spoken at the 1956 Republican Convention, Cole switched to the Democrats, supporting the campaign of the future President, John F Kennedy. In office, JFK and his successor, Lyndon Johnson, both frequently consulted Nat on civil rights issues.

His first marriage to Nadine Robinson, in 1936, ended in divorce in 1948. In almost indecent haste, some nine days later, he married Maria (born Marie) Hawkins, whose stage name was Maria Ellington, a singer with the Duke Ellington band. Their family included the adopted Carol, known as Cookie, daughter of Maria's youngest sister who died, in 1949. Their first natural child Natalie was born in 1950: she later became a moderately successful singer in her own right. In 1959, Nat and Maria adopted a boy, Kelly, followed in January 1961 by the birth of natural twin girls, Casey and Timolin. Nat's serial affairs plagued their marriage but Maria stayed true to her husband, and was with him when he died from lung cancer, on February 15 1965. Having smoked three packs of Kool menthol cigarettes a day, Nat had been convinced that smoking had kept his voice in good trim.

LEFT
Nat King Cole with his Jazz Orchestra, 1950.

BELOW
Nat King Cole pictured in the 1950s.

PERRY
COMO

Birth name: Pierino Ronald Como
Born: May 18 1912, Canonsburg, Pennsylvania
Died: May 12 2001, Jupiter Inlet Colony, Florida
Years active: 1933 to 1994
Record label(s): Decca, RCA Victor

One of the most successful performers of the twentieth century, with 27 of his records going gold and 14 number one hits, Perry Como sold more than 100 million records in a career spanning over 60 years.

Perry was born the middle child of 13 to immigrant parents from Palena, Italy. His father Pietro Como, a mill worker, and his mother Lucia Travaglini Como strove to bring up their extensive brood. Perry helped the family finances by working after school, for a few cents each day, in a local barber's shop. This fired his ambition to open his own barber's shop, an ideal establishment for airing his vocal talents, after leaving high school. Singing engagements at local weddings and other events followed, the fees received helping to pay for music lessons on the baritone horn and organ. Somewhat a rarity for his time, Como's ability to read music stood him in good stead.

In 1933, while on vacation in Cleveland, Ohio, Perry was hired to sing with the Freddie Carlone band for the princely sum of $25 a week. The salary was put to good use when he married his sweetheart from high school, Roselle Belline, the daughter of a French immigrant family. Unlike many of his contemporaries, Como's marriage was an enduring partnership that lasted until the death of Roselle, in August 1998, the year of their 65th wedding anniversary. An intensely private family, they brought up their three children away from the glare of the show business spotlight.

After becoming vocalist with the Ted Weems orchestra, Perry's popularity increased such that, when the Weems orchestra disbanded in the early 1940s, he was offered a contract by NBC to share star billing with Jo Stafford on their Chesterfield Supper Club weeknight radio show. This show was televised later in the 1940s, and the exposure revealed Como's modest and captivating personality to the viewing public. A makeover, that exchanged his usual attire of a business suit for the more casual cardigan, complemented his homely, relaxed style. A brief flirtation as a movie actor, in which he made three films, *Something for the Boys* (1944), *Doll Face* (1945) and *If I'm Lucky* (1946), with co-star Carmen Miranda, led the honest Como to admit, "I was wasting their time, and they were wasting mine."

His television shows were a different matter; his friendly persona and light baritone voice endeared him to his audiences in a series that lasted for many years, a five-year contract with CBS, in 1950, being followed by eight years with NBC. His Christmas specials for ABC-TV became an integral part of the American holidays until the late 1980s. His recordings ranged from sublime ballads, including the hit that reflected his personal

LITTLE BOOK OF CROONERS

life in its title, "No Other Love," and, the atmospheric, "Its Impossible," to the ridiculous novelty songs, "Hot Diggity Dog Ziggity Boom," and "How Much Is That Doggy In The Window?" He even made a rock-and-roll record, "Juke Box Baby," but his legacy was in the number of tuneful ballads that he recorded in his laid-back style. Perry Como has taken his place in musical history as the first vocalist to have made 10 records that each sold over one million copies. His wartime musical achievements were recognised in the 1946 award by *Billboard* magazine, as being the top-selling male singer. In 1958, the Recording Industry Association of America formally certified Como's hit single record, "Catch a Falling Star," as its first ever Gold Record. His last Top 40 hit was a cover version of the Don Maclean song, "And I Love You So", recorded in 1973 and nominated for a Grammy award that same year.

LEFT
Perry Como in the recording studio, 1953.

BELOW
Perry Como performing on stage in the 1960s.

His self-deprecating manner tended to make him play down his achievements. Sales of millions of records seemed of little consequence to him, as he continually strove for perfection in his life's work, be it in the recording studio or on his television shows. He once said, "People have always thought that I wasn't ambitious. They judged by appearances and were fooled. I was competitive. I wanted success and was willing to work for it." This was summed up in New Statesman, after his death in 2001, by a critic who wrote, "Nobody else was so intensely relaxed."

Perry Como spent the later years of his life with his lifelong sweetheart Roselle, at their home in Jupiter Inlet Colony, Florida, playing golf, fishing, and going for walks with his wife. His tireless work for charity fundraising, on golf days and on radio shows, continued until the combination of old age and ill health brought an end to his activities. After his death, the Washington Post tribute included the words, "What Perry Como did week after week on his TV shows was not so much as sing to his fans as to have a continuing conversation with them, a conversation in song."

HARRY
CONNICKJR

Birth name: Joseph Harry Fowler Connick
Born: September 11 1967, New Orleans, Louisiana
Years active: 1980s – present
Record label(s): Columbia Records

With a number of major career successes that have brought recognition from across all branches of show business, including several platinum and gold records, Grammy, Tony, and Emmy awards, and nominations for an Oscar and a Golden Globe, Harry Connick Jr has established himself as one of America's greatest entertainers.

Born in New Orleans on September 11 1967, as Joseph Harry Fowler Connick, young Harry was fortunate to be born in a city with a great musical heritage. His parents were both successful in the legal profession: his Irish Catholic father, Harry Connick Sr, became the district attorney of New Orleans between 1977 and 2003; his mother Anita, from a New York Jewish family, became a justice in the Louisiana Supreme Court. Both parents loved music, and owned a record store. His mother used to sing to Harry when he was young, stimulating his interest in music from an early age.

A precocious musician, Harry learned to play the piano by the age of three, made his first public performance when he was six, and recorded an album, *Dixieland Plus*, with a local jazz band at the age of 10. With jazz clubs often staying open late at night, his father used to drive him to the venue, late in the evening, and collect him in the small hours of the morning. His musical talent was further developed at the New Orleans Center for the Creative Arts. After high school, Harry went to study at the City University of New York, and continued his musical education at the Manhattan School of Music. While at music school, he signed his recording contract with Columbia Records.

His first recording for Columbia was an album of instrumental standards entitled *Harry Connick Jr*. Playing in jazz clubs, and other New York showcases, further served to enhance Connick's reputation. His second album was released in November 1988 with the simple title *20*, his age at the time of recording. The album featured his vocal talent with performances of songs such as, "Blue Skies," "Lazy River," and "S'Wonderful."

His reputation became such that movie director, Rob Reiner, asked Harry to provide the soundtrack for his 1989 romantic comedy film, *When Harry Met Sally.* This he did, and the soundtrack album, featuring standards like, "It Had To be You," "Don't Get Around Much Anymore," and "Let's Call the Whole Thing Off," was a major seller, achieving double-platinum status in the US. He also won his first *Grammy* for Best Jazz Male Vocal Performance for his work on the film.

The dawning of his film-acting career came in 1990, when Harry appeared in the World War 2 drama *Memphis Belle,* in which he played a crewman in a B-17 bomber. His

LITTLE BOOK OF CROONERS

part in *Little Man Tate,* in 1991, directed by Jodie Foster, was followed in 1995 with a convincing appearance as a homicidal killer in *Copycat.* His place in movies was cemented the following year, when he appeared alongside Will Smith in the blockbuster film, *Independence Day.*

Connick released two albums in 1990; a jazz album, *Lofty's Roach Soufflé,* and an album of standards, *We Are in Love,* which won double-platinum, and brought his second *Grammy* for Best Jazz Male Vocal. He also set out on a two-year world tour. Further multi-platinum success came in 1991, with his self-penned album *Blue Light, Red Light.* A solo piano album, *25,* also won platinum in the following year.

In December 1992, Harry was arrested at JFK airport, New York, when he was found to be in possession of a 9mm pistol. After spending a day in jail, he was given a conditional discharge, and made a television commercial warning viewers not to break firearm laws.

He married a Texan model, Jill Goodacre, in 1994, with whom he has three daughters. That year saw a temporary change in his musical direction that was not popular with all of his fans, with Harry releasing an album of New Orleans 'funk' music: it won a platinum award. He toured the UK and China, where his show was televised. The next 10 years brought more movie roles, a big band music album, *Come By Me,* in 1999, and a world tour. He wrote the score for the Broadway musical *Thou Shalt Not,* for which he received a Tony award. An ABC network television broadcast of *South Pacific,* co-starring Glen Close, and a gold record Christmas album, *Harry for the Holidays,* added to his growing list of achievements.

Harry was very much involved in the rebuilding plans for the victims of Hurricane Katrina that devastated his native city in 2005, and was honorary chairman of the charity, Operation Home Delivery. While his latest rescue mission has been to revive the judging panel of American Idol, the reality-singing competition series created by Simon Fuller, which was floundering until Harry joined the judges.

LEFT
Harry Connick Jr performs during the 2002 Winter Olympics Closing Ceremony.

BELOW
The versatile and talented Harry Connick Jr in 2001.

LITTLE BOOK OF CROONERS

BING CROSBY

Birth name: Harry Lillis Crosby
Born: May 3 1903, Tacoma, Washington
Died: October 14 1977, La Morajela golf course, near Madrid, Spain
Years active: 1920s – 1960s
Record label(s): Brunswick, Decca, Reprise, RCA Victor, Verve, United Artists

Considered by many to have been among the most talented singers of his generation, Bing Crosby was also one of the biggest selling recording artists of all time. With total record sales estimated at between 500 million and 900 million, and over 360 records in the charts of which 38 reached the No 1 position, his popularity, as a recording artist, is unquestionable. A successful radio and film career, and a business acumen that earned substantial returns on his investments made Bing a very wealthy man. However, there was a dark side to his personality.

Harry Lillis Crosby was born in Tacoma, Washington State, on May 3 1903, the fourth of seven children. His Anglo-American father, Harry Lowe Crosby, and his Irish-American mother, Catherine Harrigan Crosby, moved the family to Spokane, Washington, to seek work, in 1906. The name 'Bing' is believed to have been a contraction of the nickname Bingo, given to him at the age of six by a neighbour, after a character in a newspaper feature article.

At 17, a summer job in a Spokane theatre gave him the opportunity to see great acts, including the legendary Al Jolson. In 1920, Bing went to Gonzaga College, in Spokane, to study law. While at college he bought a drum-set and later joined a college band. The band made money, so Bing dropped his studies to follow a musical career. When the band broke up, Crosby headed for Los Angeles where, together with the former bandleader Al Rinker, they got singing jobs in movie theatres. The duo had already made their first recording "I've Got The Girl," when bandleader Paul Whiteman signed them, in 1926, to sing with his band. They were later fired after adverse audience reaction in New York, so Bing, Al and Harry Barris formed the Rhythm Boys, with Bing soon becoming front man.

Mack Sennett signed Bing for the musical, *I Surrender Dear*. Another five movies led to the break-up of the trio, so Crosby went solo. In the 1930s, Bing's career took off, not only in records, but also on the radio and in films, of which he made 79 in all. His popularity grew during World War 2, starting with his biggest hit record, "White Christmas," from the 1941 film, *Holiday Inn*. It has sold over 100 million copies world-wide: this total still rising. Crosby performed for US troops in Europe, and made propaganda broadcasts in German, earning him the nickname 'Der Bingle' from his German listeners. An Academy Award for Best Actor, in the film *Going My Way* in 1944, followed by many more film successes in the *'Road…'* series with Bob Hope, complemented his recording and radio achievements, culminating in a *Grammy* Lifetime Achievement Award in 1962.

LITTLE BOOK OF CROONERS

Bing Crosby played a major role in the introduction of recording tape, to replace the metallic discs that had hitherto been used for editing and broadcasting recorded programmes. In order to help perfect his radio shows, Bing invested $50,000 of his own money in the Ampex company to further the development of magnetic tape technology that would both facilitate programme editing and allow longer recordings to be made. These improvements would reduce programme-recording time that Bing could better use to pursue his golf and horseracing interests.

Crosby was twice married: his first wife, actress/singer Dixie Lee, whom he married in 1930, bore him four sons. Dixie, an alcoholic for many years, died from ovarian cancer in 1952. Bing's second marriage in 1957, to actress Kathryn Grant, 30 years his junior, brought two more sons and a daughter. Rumours, later confirmed in a book by Gary, his son from the first marriage, had Crosby accused of meanness, child beating, and psychological abuse. Bob Hope often referred to Bing's parsimonious nature, publicly. Crosby's strange attitude towards his children from the first marriage was shown in his legacy to his four sons. His will stipulated that, apart from a small allowance, they would not receive their trust fund inheritance until they were in their eighties; none survived long enough to collect, two of his sons having committed suicide after battling alcoholism and failed careers. At his death, Bing Crosby's wealth was estimated at over $150 million.

His youngest son, Nathaniel Crosby, was a top amateur golfer and the youngest winner, aged 19, of the US Amateur Championship in 1981. Bing's love of sport was reflected in his part-ownership of the Pittsburgh Pirates baseball team, from 1946 to the mid-1960s, and part-ownership of horses and racing stables in California and Argentina. Bing sold his horseracing assets in 1953, to pay off taxes owed by his first wife's estate.

Bing died on the golf course at La Morajela, near Madrid, Spain, from a massive heart attack after completing 18 holes: previous medical advice from his doctor had warned him to play only nine in future.

VIC DAMONE

Birth name: Vito Rocco Farinola
Born: June 12 1928, Brooklyn, New York
Years active: Late 1940s – 1990s
Record label(s): Mercury, Columbia, Capitol, RCA

H aving parents with an interest in music is a decided advantage to an aspiring singer. Vic Damone was no exception. His electrician father, Rocco, both sang and played guitar, and his mother Mamie was a piano teacher. This background could not have been a more fortuitous one for the young Vito Rocco Farinola, who was born in the Brooklyn district of New York on June 12 1928. At a very early age he began to mimic his favourite singer, Frank Sinatra, and also took singing lessons and voice coaching.

His father was injured at work while the young Vic was still in his teens. With no other means of supporting the family, Vic had to drop out of school and seek paid work. He found employment as an usher and lift operator in the Paramount Theatre in Manhattan. While at the theatre, he performed for Perry Como in the star's dressing room. Como liked what he had heard and referred Vic to a local bandleader, in order that he could gain experience as a performer. It was around this time that he took his mother's surname, Damone, for his stage name.

In April 1947, Damone entered the competition to find new talent on the weekly radio show *Arthur Godfrey's Talent Scouts*, which he duly won, earning himself the prize of a regular spot on that show. *Talent Scouts* was renowned over the years for showcasing artists such as Tony Bennett, Eddie Fisher, Steve Lawrence and Al Martino. Other notables who auditioned for the show, but were not chosen to appear, were Buddy Holly and Elvis Presley. At the radio station he met the actor and comedian Milton Berle, who had a vast range of show business contacts: using these led to Berle finding some regular appearances at two New York night-clubs for Damone. By the summer of 1947, Vic was given a recording contract with Mercury Records.

His first two releases for Mercury, "I Have But One Heart" and "You Do," were released in 1947 and both achieved the No 7 placing on the *Billboard* charts. More hit records followed, leading to Vic being given his own weekly radio show in 1948, *Saturday Night Serenade.* By 1951, the movies had beckoned, with Vic making two films that year for MGM, a drama starring Mickey Rooney, *The Strip*, in which Vic played himself, and the musical *Rich, Young and Pretty* opposite Jane Powell. This musical was the first of several made by Damone for MGM that include *Athena* (1953), *Deep In My Heart* (1954) and, perhaps the best of the bunch, *Kismet* (1955).

A prolific recording artist, 39 of his releases made the *Billboard* charts, with two of them, "Again" and "You're Breaking My Heart" (both in 1949) winning him gold records. His

LITTLE BOOK OF CROONERS

baritone voice was used to good effect on a range of romantic ballads from musical films including *Gigi*, and also on the more upbeat songs "Tzena, Tzena, Tzena" and "My Truly, Truly Fair."

With the prospect of two years in the US Army from 1951-53 on the horizon, Vic recorded a number of songs that were released while he served Uncle Sam. After military duty, he married the actress Pier Angeli in 1954, a short-lived union that was dissolved in 1958. Apart from the film *Kismet*, his career took a downward slide in 1955, with his only record placement in the charts, "Por Favor," reaching No 73. Early in the following year he lost his contract with Mercury, then was signed by Columbia for whom he had the hits "On the Street Where You Live" (from *My Fair Lady*), and the title song from the film *An Affair To Remember*.

A series of guest host appearances on television shows kept Vic in the public eye for a few years but, in 1960, he made what was to be his last feature film, *Hell To Eternity*, a wartime action drama about a heroic US marine. A year later, he was released by Columbia Records and joined Capitol, who had lost Frank Sinatra when he left to be one of the founders of the Reprise label. Leaving Capitol, where he had made some of his best albums, he moved to the Warner Brothers label in 1965. There he had one chart success, "You Were Only Fooling (While I Was Falling In Love)," before moving labels again, this time to RCA, where he released his last record for more than 20 years.

Beset by bankruptcy in the early 1970s, Damone sang in Las Vegas, and toured both the US and the UK to help restore his financial status. He married his current wife, fashion designer Rena Rowan in 1992. Many of Vic's recent compilation albums have sold well, and have brought the work of this fine singer to the attention of a new generation of music lovers.

BOBBY DARIN

Birth name: Walden Robert Cassotto
Born: May 14, 1936, Bronx, New York, US
Died: December 20, 1973, Los Angeles, US
Years active: 1956 - 1973
Record label(s): Decca, Atco, Capitol, Brunswick, Atlantic, Motown

obby Darin might have had more of a long-lasting reputation as a crooner had he not sung in so many different genres including pop, rock'n'roll, jazz, folk and country and also enjoyed a successful acting career.

However, he deserves to be featured in the elite list not only for his recording of "Mack The Knife" but also because of his lanquid singing style and great musical talent.

Bobby started as a songwriter in the legendary Brill Building where he was introduced to singer Connie Francis, for whom he helped write several songs. They had an affair of which her father did not approve, and the couple soon split up, a decision she said she regretted all of her life.

His career finally took off in 1958 when he recorded "Splish Splash" which he co-wrote with radio DJ Murray Kaufman after his mother, Jean, a frustrated songwriter, had suggested the title to him, and the novelty single went on to sell a million copies.

Bobby continued to make a splash with the self-penned, "Dream Lover", a ballad that became a multi-million seller in 1959. His next single, "Mack the Knife", the standard from Kurt Weill's Threepenny Opera, was given a vamping jazz-pop interpretation and although Bobby had qualms about releasing it as a single it stayed at number one on the charts for nine weeks, sold two million copies, and won the Grammy Award for Record of the Year in 1960.

Bobby followed "Mack" with "Beyond the Sea", a jazzy English-language version of Charles Trenet's French hit "La Mer". Both tracks were produced by Atlantic founder Ahmetand Ertegün with staff producer Jerry Wexler.

The late 1950s were a period of incredible success for Bobby. His charm and good looks saw him break the all-time attendance record at the Copacabana nightclub in Manhattan and headlining at the major casinos in Las Vegas.

In the early 1960s bobby began to write and sing country music, with hit songs including "Things", "You're the Reason I'm Living" and "18 Yellow Roses". In 1966, he had his final UK top ten single, with a version of Tim Hardin's "If I Were A Carpenter".

Concurrent with his singing and song writing skills was a commendable acting career. His first major film, Come September (1960), was a teenager-oriented romantic comedy with 18-year old actress Sandra Dee. They first met during the production of the film, fell in love, and got married soon afterwards.

In 1963, he was nominated for an Academy Award for Best Supporting Actor for his

LITTLE BOOK OF CROONERS

role as a shell-shocked soldier in Captain Newman, M.D.. At the Cannes Film Festival he won the French Film Critics Award for best actor.

Throughout the 1960s, he became more politically active and worked on Robert Kennedy's Democratic presidential campaign. He was present on the night of June 4, 1968, at the Ambassador Hotel in Los Angeles at the time of Kennedy's assassination.

The same year, he discovered that he had been brought up by his grandparents, not his parents, and that the girl he thought was his sister was actually his mother! These events deeply affected Bobby and sent him into a long period of seclusion.

Although he made a successful television comeback, his health was beginning to fail, as he had always expected, following bouts of rheumatic fever in childhood. This knowledge of his vulnerability had always spurred him on to exploit his musical talent while still young.

He died on December 20, 1973, at the early age of 37, following a heart operation in Los Angeles. He once said, " My goal is to be remembered as a human being and as a great performer ". Few would argue that he didn't live up to this ambition.

SAMMY
DAVIS JR

Birth name: Samuel George Davis, Jr
Born: December 8 1925, Harlem, New York
Died: May 16 1990, Beverly Hills, California
Years active: 1930s – 1980s
Record label(s): Brunswick, Decca, Capitol, Reprise, Motown, United Artists

From his early years in vaudeville, to the casino theatres of Las Vegas, the career of Sammy Davis, Jr ranged from song-and-dance man, Broadway show performer, film actor, recording star and cabaret artist. At times a controversial personality, he was a political activist who made a major impact in the struggle against racism in the US, as he played a prominent role in the civil rights movement.

Samuel George Davis, Jr was born in the Harlem district of New York on December 8 1925. His father, Sammy Davis, Sr was an African-American vaudeville entertainer, as was his mother, Elvera Sanchez, a Cuban-American. His parents were often on the road so his grandmother brought up Sammy. At the age of three, Sammy's parents separated; his father, anxious not to lose custody, took the youngster with him on tour. There, he learned to dance with his father and the man he called 'uncle', Will Mastin, and soon, when still a child, became a member of the Will Mastin Trio, forging a lifelong bond between them. This bond existed to the extent that, even after Sammy Jr had gone solo, he still gave the trio billing on his show, and paid his father and Will a generous percentage of his earnings.

The two older men both played a large part in protecting the young Sammy from the overt racism that existed in the US at the time. It came as a great shock to him when, while serving in the US Army during World War 2, Sammy Jr came into first-hand contact with racial prejudice. He later used his talent as an army entertainer to deflect some of the racist hatred, hoping to bridge the void between cultural differences. After the war he rejoined the trio, as well as working on his solo career. In 1949, he recorded his first of many albums and singles. His treatment of songs from the shows later earned him a major role in Mr Wonderful on Broadway in 1956.

A car crash in 1954 left him without his left eye. In hospital, he learned of the similarities between the Jewish and Black cultures, and the intolerance both races had suffered, from his friend Eddie Cantor. Sammy converted to Judaism around this time. His inner strength and resolve against racism was put to the test when, in 1960, he married the white Swedish actress, May Britt. Sammy endured threats against his life from white extremist groups, leading to the early closure of his *Tony*-nominated performance in the Broadway musical, *Golden Boy*, in the mid-1960s. An admitted affair with singer Lola Falana, one of many women in his life, led to divorce in 1968. In the same year, he began dating a dancer from the show *Golden Boy*, Altovise Gore, who he married in 1970, the wedding ceremony being conducted by the Reverend Jesse Jackson.

LITTLE BOOK OF CROONERS

Davis joined the fight against prejudice that allowed black people to perform in hotels and casinos in Las Vegas, but not to rent rooms there. As his star status grew, Sammy and other top black performers refused to appear at venues where racial segregation existed, resulting in the eventual integration of premises in both Miami Beach and Las Vegas.

In 1959, Davis became a member of the group originally known as 'The Clan' led by his friend Frank Sinatra. Sammy objected to the name 'Clan', with its racist connotation, so it became 'The Summit', but was more commonly known as the 'Rat Pack'. His association brought accusations and innuendo suggesting that Sammy had Mafia connections, along with some of his fellow members.

Sammy Davis, Jr was a tireless workaholic, often putting his acting, television and recording work before family obligations. A long-time heavy drinker, he gradually became addicted to cocaine. His use of drugs caused him to be shunned by his friend Sinatra, who despised narcotic users. They were reconciled after Sammy gave up drugs; however, he remained a chain-smoker, which had earned him his Rat Pack sobriquet, Smokey; it would eventually cost him his life.

In 1961, although a confirmed Democratic voter, Davis felt snubbed by the White House, after being removed from the list of performers at JF Kennedy's inauguration celebrations. He believed this was because of his inter-racial marriage, a political thorn in the side of the US ruling party. Within 10 years, Sammy was wholeheartedly supporting the Republican candidate, Richard Nixon, and was widely criticised for it within the black community.

Davis worked in cabaret, television, and recorded for Motown during the 70s and 80s. His death from throat cancer, in 1990, left his widow Altovise with the task of selling off much of his memorabilia to settle his estate that owed over $7.5 million in unpaid taxes. Over 10 years after his death, he was given a *Grammy* Lifetime Achievement Award.

LEFT
Sammy Davis Jr performing in the 60s.

BELOW
Sammy Davis Jr skips to his Rolls Royce, whilst in London, 1963.

SACHA **DISTEL**

Birth name: Alexandre Distel
Born: January 29, 1933, Paris, France
Died: July 22, 2004, Rayol-Canadel, France
Years active: 1948 - 2004
Record label(s): Atlantic, Philips, RCA Victor, Warner Bros, Mercury

S acha Distel probably saw himself more of a jazz musician than a crooner but will forever be remembered for his cover version of the Academy Award-winning "Raindrops Keep Falling On My Head" .

Sacha was the son of Russian White émigré Leonid Distel whose uncle, Ray Ventura, was a jazz promoter and band-leader who pioneered the development of swing in France. Sacha had trained as a pianist but when he heard the jazz trumpeter Dizzy Gillespie's first Paris concert in 1948, it proved a revelation – and he promptly abandoned piano for the guitar.

Ventura's band had many of the best instrumentalists in France in its line-up, and in his teens Sacha started to take lessons with the famous guitarist and composer Henri Salvador. In 1951, Sacha won first prize in a nationwide competition for guitar, and went on to hold the top place three years running.

His first visit to New York, in 1952, proved another inspiration. The fusion of modern American jazz and the post-war style of French song - what became known as the Saint Germain sound - suited Sacha's talents. He accompanied Juliette Gréco, the greatest chanteuse of the day, and also worked with Georges Brassens, for many the most inspired songwriter-singer of the 1950s.

Sacha made his first recordings as an instrumentalist in the middle of that decade, with Lionel Hampton ("French New Sound") and the Modern Jazz Quartet ("Afternoon In Paris"). A short-lived romance with Brigitte Bardot in 1958 put his photograph on the cover of every French fan magazine, and shortly afterwards he began his career as a vocalist. One of his first singles was a tribute to Bardot, entitled "Brigitte À Jamais".

It was the French version of an American hit, "Scoubidou", in 1959, that catapulted Sacha to the top. The song became what one historian called "L'hymne de la jeunesse en France". Dozens of other songs followed, among them "O Quelle Nuit", "Personnalités", "Mon Beau Chapeau", "Le Boogie Du Bébé", "Scandale Dans La Famille", "Ces Mots Stupides" and "L'Incendie À Rio". In 1967, he recorded Stevie Wonder's "You Are The Sunshine" with Bardot, as "Le Soleil De Ma Vie".

In the 1970s, he became popular outside France, and once hosted the Miss World contest in London. During this decade, he spent more time in the UK than in France. His only British hit single came in 1970 with a cover of "Raindrops Keep Falling On My Head", the Oscar- winning Burt Bacharach/Hal David song from the Western Butch Cassidy and the Sundance Kid. Sacha's version reached No.10 in the UK while the original recording by B. J.

LITTLE BOOK OF CROONERS

Thomas, a million-seller in the US, had been only a minor British chart entry.

Sacha appeared on numerous TV variety shows in the UK throughout the 1970s and 1980s, including Seaside Special and The Val Doonican Show. Maintaining his popularity in his homeland, however, Sacha recorded French versions of various English-language million-sellers. These included "Vite, Cherie, Vite" ("Beach Baby"), "Chanson Bleue" ("Song Sung Blue") and "Je T'Appelle Pour Dire Que Je T'Aime" ("I Just Called To Say I Love You"). He also recorded in German, Spanish and Italian to satisfy his audiences in other parts of Europe.

In August 1980, in honour of Queen Elizabeth The Queen Mother, Sacha performed at Buckingham Palace to mark her 80th birthday. The Queen Mother was said to have been impressed by Sacha's moving voice and later in the night she requested "You Must Have Been a Beautiful Baby", a song that had been recorded by Perry Como, one of her favourite singers.

Sacha remained popular in France in the 1980s and 1990s, with a new show named after his song "La Belle Vie". In 2000, Sacha had a part as lawyer Billy Flynn in the London production of Chicago.

Married to championship Olympic skier Francine Bréaud in 1963, Sacha publicly stated that he remained faithful to his wife, saying "Anything I want in a woman I can get at home." They had two sons and lived in Ovington, Northumberland for a short time in the 1980s and 90s

Sacha died on 22 July 2004, aged 71, after a long illness, in Rayol-Canadel, southeast France. Just two weeks before his death, he could be seen on TV participating in a charity broadcast – a trouper to the end.

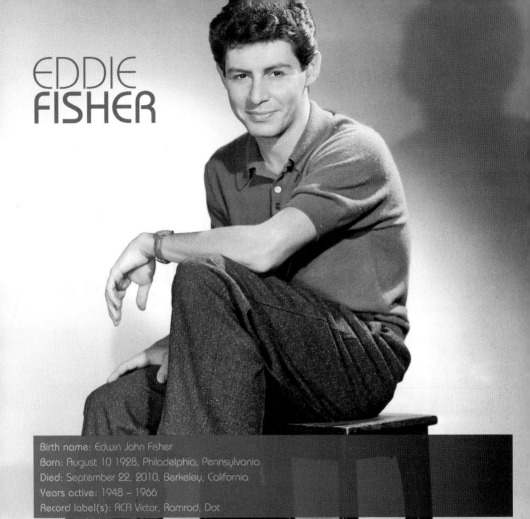

EDDIE
FISHER

Birth name: Edwin John Fisher
Born: August 10 1928, Philadelphia, Pennsylvania
Died: September 22, 2010, Berkeley, California
Years active: 1948 – 1966
Record label(s): RCA Victor, Ramrod, Dot

During the 1950s, Eddie Fisher was, along with Perry Como and Elvis Presley, one of RCA Victor's top three best-selling recording stars. His comparatively short career was carried out in the spotlight of public attention, famous not only for his singing but also his high-profile matrimonial affairs, alcoholism, drug addiction and gambling. With candid honesty, he never shied away from admitting to his personal failings although, according to his autobiography, some of his wives were not entirely free from blame, either.

Edwin John Fisher was born in the City of Brotherly Love, Philadelphia, on August 10 1928 to Joseph and Kate Fisher, the fourth of their seven children. His parents were of Russian-Jewish origin where their surname was believed to have originally been 'Fisch', but became Fisher during the immigration process. The young Eddie was known within the family circle as Sonny Boy. Still very young when his talent as a singer became apparent, he was soon entering, and often winning, amateur talent contests.

While at high school, he performed on a local radio show, then later appeared on the network radio talent show that had unearthed many well-known entertainers in the 1940s, *Arthur Godfrey's Talent Scouts*. By the age of 18, Fisher was crooning with the big-name bands of Buddy Morrow and Charlie Ventura. His career took off when, at the age of 21, he was spotted by Eddie Cantor, who gave him exposure on Cantor's nationally networked radio programme. He was an immediate hit, and was soon rewarded with a recording contract by RCA Victor.

Called up for service with the US Army in 1951, Eddie spent a year in Korea before being drafted into the US Army Chorus, in Washington DC. Although conscripted, patriotic publicity pictures of him wearing army uniform gave his career a boost after demobilisation. He was given star billing as a singer in top night-clubs and, within the next four years, had two television series of his own, as well as making guest appearances on others.

His recording career was a great success, with Eddie becoming one of the most popular singers of the 1950s. In the first six years of that decade, he had 17 records in the Top 10 charts and 35, in total, that made the Top 40. Three reached the coveted No 1 position, "Wish You Were Here" (1952), "Oh My Pa-Pa," a million-seller in 1953, and a duet with Sally Sweetland also in 1953, "I'm Walking Behind You." His television achievements brought him a Golden Globe award in 1957.

An idol of American teenagers, especially the girls, he made his film debut, starring with his wife Debbie Reynolds, whom he had married late in 1955, in the 1956 musical

LITTLE BOOK OF CROONERS

comedy *Bundle of Joy*. He also played a serious role in *Butterfield 8*, in which his then wife Elizabeth Taylor was the female lead.

His great friend, producer and entrepreneur Mike Todd, who was the husband of Elizabeth Taylor, was killed in a plane crash in 1958. Fisher's subsequent affair with Todd's widow caused a major Hollywood scandal that led to a messy and very public divorce from Debbie in 1959, leaving him free to marry Taylor that same year. This marriage lasted until 1965, and was followed by a two-year marriage to actress Connie Stevens from 1967-69. An even shorter marriage to Terry Richard in 1975 ended in divorce the following year. He was married for the fifth time in 1993 to Betty Lin, the union lasting until her death from cancer in 2001. Fisher has admitted affairs with many other women, and has documented these in his second autobiography, published in 1981, *Eddie: My Life, My Loves*.

After his career as a recording artist stalled in the late 1950s, Eddie released his live recorded album, *Eddie Fisher at the Winter Garden*, on his own label Ramrod. He rejoined RCA in the mid-1960s and made three albums, *Games That Lovers Play, People Like You* and *You Ain't Heard Nothin' Yet*. In 1965, his album release on the Dot label, *Eddie Fisher Today*, reached only No 72 on the album charts, with a mixture of standards and songs from the shows. Three more albums, *When I Was Young, Mary Christmas,* and *Young and Foolish,* were also released in 1965 on the Dot label, and a greatest hits album in 1968. Although not chart-toppers, these releases brought in a few more dollars but effectively signalled the end of Fisher as a recording artist.

Towards the end of his performing career, he made few recordings but continued to sing at venues around the US. He suffered from health problems in later life and rarely appeared in public. After breaking his hip, he died in September 2010 at his Californian home due to complications from hip surgery. His second, and most-famous wife, Elizabeth Taylor, died six months and one day after Eddie, on March 23, 2011.

ENGELBERT
HUMPERDINCK

Birth name: Arnold George Dorsey
Born: May 2 1936, Madras, India
Years active: Early 1950s – present
Record label(s): Decca, Mercury, London, Epic, Columbia, Varesse, Image

I n over 40 years at the top of the entertainment business, one man has defined the world of romance in song, having sold more than 130 million records, including 64 gold and 24 platinum albums. With a stage name that was originally a publicity-seeking gimmick, Engelbert Humperdinck has become one of the world's greatest entertainers. His voice, coupled with his warm personality and great sense of humour, has endeared him to his millions of fans from all over the world.

Arnold George Dorsey was born in Madras, India, on May 2 1936, the youngest boy of three and seven girls. His father was serving in the British forces and had met his Indian-born wife while serving on the sub-continent. The family moved to England in 1946 and settled in the Leicester area. The young Arnold became interested in music and, at the age of 11 years, began to study the saxophone. In his mid-teens, while playing saxophone at a pub talent contest his friends, who knew of his talent for mimicry, persuaded him to enter the show with his vocal impression of Jerry Lewis. He soon acquired the name Gerry as his stage name, and started singing in night-clubs until military service placed his professional career on hold for two years.

Back in civilian life in 1958, he was signed by Decca but his only single release, "I'll Never Fall in Love Again," failed to sell. Dorsey continued performing until 1961, when he was stricken with tuberculosis that could have ended his career and possibly, his life. In 1965, a meeting with an old roommate, promoter and manager Gordon Mills, was to have an impact on his future career, as well as bringing another change of name. The astute Mills realised that, in order to make the grade in the music industry against the highly competitive rock music groups of the day, a stage name that was both distinctive and unforgettable was needed. He first persuaded Dorsey that the name of the German composer, Engelbert Humperdinck, would fit both requirements, and also secured a record deal with Decca.

In 1967, his recording of "Release Me" achieved a major success for Engelbert, rapidly reaching the No 1 position in the British charts, selling up to 85,000 copies daily, and famously beating the Beatles' "Strawberry Fields Forever" to that spot. Similar success followed in the American charts, firmly imprinting the name of Humperdinck in the minds of the record-buying public, particularly those of the female gender. His career took off in the late 1960s and early 70s, selling millions of records of love songs, and starring in stage shows at the rate of around 100 performances in a year. At one time, his

fan club was claimed to have the largest membership of any similar organisation in the world, over eight million, all potential record buyers and every one of them eager for Engelbert's next record release.

In the 1970s, as popular music moved into another style, his records began to sell less well than previously so Engelbert put more of his energies into his stage shows. These became more lavish and spectacular, ideally suited to the casino theatres of Las Vegas and elsewhere. His honesty and loyalty to his fans were demonstrated by his desire to give them something different from anything they might have seen before, and he has been quoted as saying, "I take the job description of 'entertainer' very seriously!"

His 1976 album, *After the Lovin'*, earned him the critical acclaim he deserved, a *Grammy* Award being his first major honour granted by the show business industry. Engelbert had been given little artistic control over his album recordings until late in the 1980s but after that time his output took on a wider appeal, although love songs still featured largely in his chosen musical content. By 1980, just a few years short of his 50th birthday, he was still making albums, performing in over 200 concerts each year, and was still a major attraction for his female fans. Through all this, he managed to maintain a close family life with his wife, Patricia, and their four children. The children are all involved in the 'family business' and the family travels frequently between their homes in Leicestershire and Beverly Hills, California.

In 1989, further honours came Humperdinck's way when he was given a star on the Hollywood Walk of Fame and a Golden Globe Award for Entertainer of the Year. Around this time, he began a continuing major involvement with charity organisations, both in Britain and the US. Still keeping up a punishing schedule in his 70s, the man with the pretentious-sounding name has been described as "… a true gentleman." His recording of "Jerusalem" was selected as the England anthem for the Rugby World Cup in 2007, and he also represented the UK in the final of the Eurovision Song Contest 2012, in Baku, Azerbaijan, where he came 25th out of 26 entries.

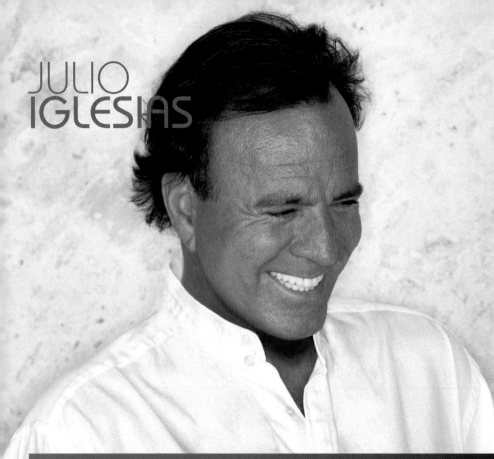

JULIO
IGLESIAS

Birth name: Julio José Iglesias de la Cueva
Born: September 23, 1943, Madrid
Years active: 1968 - present
Record label(s): Columbia Records and Sony Music Entertainment

S panish crooner Julio Iglesias has sold more than 300 million records worldwide and is reputedly the biggest selling Latin music artist of all time. Born on September 23, 1943 in Madrid, the son of Julio Iglesias Senior, one of the youngest gynaecologists in the country, he alternated between playing professional football and studying law at the CEU San Pablo University in Madrid.

In his early adulthood, he was a goalkeeper for Real Madrid but his professional football career ended when he had a serious car accident and was unable to walk for two years. Afterwards, he said of those years, "I had more courage and attitude than talent." These qualities were sorely tested when the crash smashed his lower spine; his legs were permanently weakened as a direct result and they still required therapy several years later. During his hospitalization after the accident, a nurse gave him a guitar so that he might have something to do with his hands. In learning to play, he discovered he also had a great singing voice. After his recovery, Julio studied for three months at language school in Cambridge, before going back to obtain his law degree at Complutense University of Madrid.

In 1968, he entered and won the Benidorm International Song Festival with the song "La vida Sigue Igual" (meaning "Life Goes On The Same") which helped him secure a record deal with Discos Columbia, the Spanish branch of the Columbia Records company. He represented Spain in the 1970 Eurovision Song Contest, finishing in fourth place with the song "Gwendolyne", behind Ireland's winning entry performed by Dana.

Shortly after he had a number one hit in many European countries with "Un Canto A Galicia." particularly in Germany where it sold one million copies. In 1975 he found success in the Italian market by recording a song exclusively in Italian called "Se mi lasci non vale" ("If You Leave Me, It Can't Be"). Notable albums from this decade include A Flor de Piel (1974), "El Amor" (1975), and "Soy" (1973). He also sang in French and one of his most popular songs is "Je n'ai pas changé".

In 1979, he moved to Miami, Florida, and signed a deal with CBS International, and started singing in different languages such as English, French, Portuguese and German. Julio released the album De Niña a Mujer (1981), dedicated to his daughter (who shared the cover photo with him) and from it came the first English-language hit, a Spanish cover of "Begin the Beguine" which reached No 1 in the UK.

In 1984, he released 1100 Bel Air Place, the hit album which established him as a star

LITTLE BOOK OF CROONERS

in the English-speaking entertainment industry. It sold more than three million albums in the US alone. The first single "To All the Girls I've Loved Before", a duet with Willie Nelson, hit No 1 on the Country charts and went Top Five in the Billboard Hot 100. It also featured "All of You", with Diana Ross, a Top 20 pop hit.

The new millennium was no less successful for Julio. His album Divorcio (2003) sold a record 350,000 albums on its first day of sale in Spain, and reached the number one spot on the charts in Spain, Portugal, France, Italy and Russia

He released an English album entitled Romantic Classics in September 2006 - "I've chosen songs from the 1960s, 1970s and 1980s that I believe will come to be regarded as the new standards" – which featured the hits "I Want to Know What Love Is", "Careless Whisper", and "Right Here Waiting".

April 2013 was a flagship month for Julio. He received two historic awards - Most Popular International Artist of All Time in China, and the Guinness World Record for the Best-selling Male Latin Artist. In that month he was also inducted into the Latin Songwriters Hall of Fame, alongside Armando Manzanero and José Feliciano.

Julio had three children from his first marriage in 1971 and after that was annulled in 1979 he remarried Dutch model Miranda Rijnsburger in August 2010 and they have five children. They live in the Dominican Republic, where Julio owns several hotel complexes as well as a share of the Punta Cana International Airport.

His father Julio Sr. died to a heart attack at the age of 90 in 2005. A week before his death it became known that his 42-year-old wife was pregnant with their second child. The children of Julio are now in the unusual position of saying 'uncle' and 'auntie' to kids who are decades younger than themselves!

JACK JONES

Birth name: John Allan Jones
Born: January 14 1938, Hollywood, California
Years active: 1957 – Mid 2000s
Record label(s): Capitol, Kapp Records (London, in the UK), RCA, MGM, Sony/Legacy, Honest Entertainment

With musical influences from artistes such as Frank Sinatra, Tony Bennett and Mel Tormé, together with a singing talent inherited from his father, it is no wonder that Jack Jones went on to record over 50 albums, of which 17 reached the Billboard Top 20. With two Grammys for his singles, "Lollipops and Roses" and "Wives and Lovers", both public and music industry alike have recognised the vocal achievements of this great singer.

The son of singer and movie actor Allan Jones and popular actress Irene Hervey, Jack was born on the same night that his father had recorded his best-known hit, "Donkey Serenade". Jack's formative years were spent as a privileged but talented scholar, first at junior school, then at University High School in Los Angeles. Although he played down his show business background, while at high school he studied drama and took private singing lessons paid for by his father. His talents were not limited to the performing arts: track and field athletics and football were among his accomplishments, although he later gave up his on-the-field activities to concentrate on the performing aspects of his education. At high school, an event took place that sowed the seed for Jack's future career plan. A friend and fellow pupil, Nancy Sinatra, persuaded her father to sing in the school theatre; this was the spark that lit the fire in Jack's ambition.

His life was turned topsy-turvy when his parents divorced and, on graduating from school, was faced with a harsher financial situation than he had ever been in before. He eventually made his debut on the professional stage when he was 19 years old. A small part in his father's act at the Thunderbird Hotel in Las Vegas gave Jack the incentive to start his own solo singing career, with other casual work helping to pay his way in life. After recording a demonstration record for songwriter Don Raye, he was signed by Capitol for whom he recorded several unsuccessful singles and an album. Although Jack had a low opinion of the album, one track impressed the owner of a San Francisco club, who gave him a three-week booking there. At that club, Pete King, a producer for Kapp Records heard him, and promptly signed Jones to that label.

Jack's reputation was enhanced by his ability to choose songs, and interpret them in a respectful and emotional manner, written by the great songwriters of the day including, Cole Porter, George and Ira Gershwin, and a particular favourite writer of his, Michel Legrand. In 1971, Jones paid the Frenchman Legrand a huge compliment by recording the first vocal album, in English, of the composer's songs. This album, *Jack Jones Sings Michel*

LITTLE BOOK OF CROONERS

Legrand, is one of the singer's personal favourites. He made records that brought more awards: his version of "Wives and Lovers" was nominated for Record of the Year, as was "The Impossible Dream".

Away from the recording studio, Jack made appearances in several lesser films, such as *The Comeback* and, more recently, in the feature-length British TV comedy *Cruise of the Gods* in which he co-starred with Steve Coogan. Over a number of years, his impact on the stage in musicals such as *Guys and Dolls, South Pacific,* and *The Pajama Game* brought him acclaim from audiences and critics alike. Theme songs from films, including "The Love Boat" gave wider exposure to his vocal talents. Touring still features on Jack's schedule, having completed a series of shows across Britain during 2006. Guest appearances on television, personal appearances and charity fund-raising all keep him active after 50 years in show business. A deserved honour came Jack's way in 1989 when he was given his own star on the Hollywood Walk of Fame, close to that of his father.

A series of well-publicised affairs and failed marriages dogged this good-looking, all-American singer throughout his life until, in 1982, he married for the fifth time, to his English-born wife Kim. This marriage has stood the test of time and the pair, with their daughter Nicole, born in 1991, now reside in Palm Springs. Nicole has appeared on stage with her father, during her school holidays, and also in her own right in local productions in Palm Springs. One of Jack's greatest friendships has been with Tony Bennett, who he met at Bennett's last night of a season at a Chicago hotel in 1960, with Jones taking over the residency from his new friend the following day. In 1998, in celebration of their friendship, Jack released a tribute album, *Jack Jones Paints A Tribute to Tony Bennett,* sung in the distinctive and stylish Jones manner. Frank Sinatra once said of Jones, "Jack is one of the major singers of our time ". He still occasionally performs and in 2013, appeared as a nightclub singer in the film American Hustle.

LITTLE BOOK OF CROONERS

FRANKIE LAINE

Birth name: Francesco Paolo LaVecchio
Born: March 13, 1913, Near West Side, Chicago, US
Died: February 6, 2007, San Diego, California, US
Years active: 1937 - 2005
Record label(s): Mercury, Philips, Columbia, Capitol, ABC, Amos, Score

In the world of popular music, yesterday's idol is very often tomorrow's forgotten name. Only a handful of performers have ever demonstrated the lasting appeal it takes to weather the onslaught of fads and changing trends over the years: Frankie Laine was a classic example. His impeccable musicianship and taste kept him an international favourite for six decades.

Ever since his recording of "That's My Desire" burst onto the scene like a musical firework in 1947, praise poured in from all corners, from young and old alike, for this gifted and versatile artist.

Frankie's magical appeal, however, far transcended mere nostalgia. His recording of "You Gave Me a Mountain," a song written especially for him by his good friend, Marty Robbins, went gold in the early 1970's, a time by which many of his contemporaries had long since quieted down.

Frankie continued to record exciting new material while maintaining a healthy respect for the songs, like "Mule Train," "That Lucky Old Sun," "I Believe," and "Jezebel," which all his long -time admirers know by heart. Many of these tunes were collected into an album entitled "The World of Frankie Laine" that topped the UK charts in 1982 and has been released in 43 different countries.

Born to immigrant parents in the heart of Chicago's Little Italy on March 30, 1913, Frankie first sang in public as part of the choir at the Church of the Immaculate Conception.

At the age of 17, Frankie left home to try his luck as a marathon dancer. This fad of the depression years was a tough way of keeping body and soul together, but he stuck with it and eventually he and a partner, Ruth Smith, broke the all-time marathon dance record in Atlantic City, New Jersey. They danced for a total of 3,501 hours over 145 consecutive days, and split a grand prize of $1,000 for their efforts.

When Frankie decided to make his living with his voice instead of his feet, the road to success proved long and hard. It led him up and down the Eastern Seaboard, when in 1946, Hoagy Carmichael heard the young unknown performing a favourite Carmichael composition, "Rocking Chair." This chance encounter led to a recording contract with Mercury Records. On his first session he recorded a forgotten 1931 ballad entitled, "That's My Desire," and from that point on, there was just no stopping Frankie.

Frankie, along with Nat King Cole, who preceded him by a year, marked the

LITTLE BOOK OF CROONERS

LITTLE BOOK OF CROONERS

ascendance of the popular singer over the Big Bands, and his phenomenal success set the pattern for Johnny Ray, Tony Bennett, Elvis Presley, Tom Jones and the other musical idols who have followed. His crooning style was thrillingly new to the audiences of the late 1940's, based as it was on his deep love of jazz and the blues.

The hit records were followed by starring roles in several motion pictures, guest appearances on numerous major radio and television shows, and his own television variety program on CBS in the mid-1950's. With a 1953 Warner Brother's production, "Blowing Wild," Frankie started something different: he became the first and most successful of the singers to be identified with title songs. To date he has performed the title songs for seven motion pictures, most recently in 1974, Mel Brooks Western farce, "Blazing Saddles." On television, Frankie's featured recording of "Rawhide" has become one of the most popular theme songs of all time.

In 1996, Frankie was presented with a Lifetime Achievement Award at the 27th Annual Songwriters Hall of Fame awards ceremony at the New York SheratonMaking his first New York appearance in more than 20 years, Frankie gave a performance to remember of "Cry of the Wild Goose" - his voice warm, robust and thrilling. With verve, he moved on to "That's My Desire," the haunting "We'll Be Together Again" and the dramatic "Jezebel," bringing the audience to its feet several times.

Twice married, Frankie died of heart failure on February 6, 2007, at Scripps Mercy Hospital in San Diego. In a prepared statement, his family said, "He will be forever remembered for the beautiful music he brought into this world, his wit and sense of humour, along with the love he shared with so many."

BARRY
MANILOW

Birth name: Barry Alan Pincus
Born: June 17 1943, Brooklyn, New York
Years active: 1970s – present
Record label(s): Bell (later Arista), RCA Records, Concord

arry Manilow has often been derided by his critics as a 'pop singer' and flamboyant showman but has, nevertheless, endeared himself to his many, largely female, fans. His musical pedigree is without question, as a writer, arranger and musical director, and as a singer of swing tunes, jazz, and evergreen ballads.

Barry Alan Pincus was born on June 17 1943. When he was only two years old, his father, Harold Pincus, left the family, so his mother Edna and Barry went to live with his Russian-Jewish maternal grandparents, Joseph and Esther Manilow. Barry made his first recording in 1948, at the age of 5 years, when he sang "Happy Birthday" that made into a 78rpm record for his grandfather, as a gift for a family member. Barry has twice used samples from this recording in albums recorded in the 1970s.

His interest in music developed when he started to play the accordion, a popular instrument around his Italian/Jewish neighbourhood, in the early 50s. When he was 13, in the year of his Bar Mitzvah, his stepfather gave him a piano as a birthday present. His mother also legally changed his surname to Manilow that same year. In the five years before he graduated from high school, he established himself as 'the' local pianist. With his eyes firmly set on achieving musical celebrity, emulating his idols, Harold Arlen, Irving Berlin and Cole Porter, Barry took a course of study at the Juilliard College of Music, New York, paying his fees with earnings from working in the post room at CBS Broadcasting.

Barry later gained employment at CBS as a musical director of the show Callback and also wrote, produced and performed radio-advertising jingles for companies like Dr Pepper, McDonalds and Kentucky Fried Chicken. He also wrote a musical score for a melodrama, *The Drunkard,* which ran for eight years. In 1964, Manilow married his sweetheart from high school, Susan Deixler, but the marriage ended in 1966, when Barry asked for a divorce.

In 1971, Bette Midler hired him as her pianist, arranger and musical director and, in the following year, was given a spot on her Carnegie Hall show, where he performed some of his own material. This led to a recording contract with the new Bell label, for which he released his less than successful debut album, *Barry Manilow 1,* in 1973. When Bell was taken over by Arista, the company asked him to record a version of "Brandy", a song that had been a hit in England for its co-writer Scott English. Manilow changed it from a pop song to a ballad, renamed it "Mandy" and, after releasing it on his 1974 album *Barry Manilow II,* it became a No 1 hit early in the next year.

LITTLE BOOK OF CROONERS

His next release hit the Top 20, followed by a Top 10 appearance with "Could It Be Magic", a single from his first album. The late 70s became Manilow's most fruitful period in record sales with his second No 1 hit, "I Write The Songs" (1976), a triple platinum album, *This One's for You,* in the same year, followed by another No 1 in 1977, "Looks Like We Made It". After several further successes, the momentum gradually slowed following his last Top 10 placement, "I Made It Through The Rain".

Although he frequented the charts on many occasions in the next few years, in 1984 Barry took a change in career direction towards jazz and swing music, with albums like *Swing Street* (1987), *Singin' With The Big Bands* (1994) and Manilow *Sings Sinatra* (1998). He also wrote and performed the stage musicals *Copacabana* (1994) and *Harmony* (1999). A change in record company to Concord, a jazz label, in 2001, heralded a return to his more popular music style. At the 2002 pre-game show for the US Super Bowl, Manilow performed a new song, "Let Freedom Ring", which brought him back into public focus as a recording artist. In March of that year, his new album, *Ultimate Manilow,* entered the album charts at No 3. A DVD of his collection was followed by a two-CD album of live performances called *2 Nights Live.* The former head of Arista, Clive Davis, produced a 2005 studio album featuring Barry singing tracks from the 1950s, called *Greatest Songs of the Fifties* that went to the top of the album charts in 2006. The latter part of 2006 saw a companion release, *Greatest Songs of the Sixties.*

After a recent 'farewell' tour, Barry showed both his sense of humour and self-deprecation when he said, "It must have been another generation that discovered me. Or maybe they were brainwashed by their parents and wanted to see me before I died. 'Look, he's still breathing. Buy the ticket!'" British fans had another chance to buy their tickets when he played London, Glasgow and Cardiff in May 2014 but they still hope and expect that he will be back!

LEFT
Barry Manilow on stage, 2007.

BELOW
Barry Manilow in concert at Wembley Arena, 1980.

DEAN
MARTIN

Birth name: Dino Paul Crocetti
Born: June 7 1917, Steubenville, Ohio
Died: December 25 1995, Beverly Hills, Los Angeles
Years active: 1940s – late 1970s
Record label(s): Capitol, Reprise

A man who could not read music recorded more than 100 albums, had many major hit singles, and also starred in movies and television shows. He became a show business icon, yet was uncomfortable in the glare of publicity and was not overly impressed with stardom. After many years in the public eye, Dean Martin became almost reclusive in his later years, particularly after losing his son, a pilot, in an air crash.

Dino Paul Crocetti was born on June 7 1917 in Steubenville, Ohio, the son of an immigrant Italian barber, Gaetano Crocetti and his wife, Angela. Dino spoke only Italian until he went to school, aged 5 years. This caused him to suffer the taunts of his fellow schoolmates for his broken English and probably accounted for his poor reading skills, recounting in later life that he had only ever read one book, Black Beauty, preferring instead, comic books that he asked others to buy for him.

A school drop-out at 15, he was employed in diverse odd jobs, from steelworker to bootleg alcohol deliveries, and also took up prize-fighting, as 'Kid Crochet', from which activity he received a little prize money, along with a broken nose. He later gave up fighting to work in an illegal casino, as a croupier, and started to sing with local bands, billed as Dino Martini. In the early 1940s, he worked with bandleader Sammy Watkins, changing his name to Dean Martin around that time. He married his first wife, Betty McDonald, with whom he had four children before their divorce in 1949.

Dean succeeded Frank Sinatra at a club in 1943; although Dean was a flop, their meeting was the start of a long acquaintance. Martin was renowned for bad money management, mainly because he was earning so little, and often sold percentages of his future earnings for cash advances. This could have been the beginning of his alleged Mafia connections. After serving for one year in the US Army, Dean was discharged on medical grounds. By 1946, he was becoming more successful as a night-club singer, but was not as popular as Sinatra, who was a major attraction. A meeting with an up-and-coming comic at a New York club, where they were both performing, was the beginning of the, later, world famous double-act, Dean Martin and Jerry Lewis. As they built their act their audiences grew, leading to them being given a radio series in 1949, followed by a film contract with Paramount, in Hollywood.

Although their Paramount contract only netted the pair $75,000 between them, a private venture with their own company York Productions, coupled with stage, radio and television shows, and recording contracts, earned the pair millions. As part of the hottest

LITTLE BOOK OF CROONERS

act in the US, Dean was adored by his many female fans who loved to watch as he sang romantic ballads, one of which, "That's Amore", became a hit in 1953. By 1956, Dean was growing tired of his partner's on-stage antics and jealousy so, after many months of work by lawyers, the partnership was dissolved.

Having made many comedy films with Lewis, a straight-acting role alongside Marlon Brando in *The Young Lions* in 1957 served to bring Dean's career back into the spotlight. Several more films and a series of hit records including "Memories Are Made of This", "Volare", and "You're Nobody Till Somebody Loves You" culminated in the record that became his theme song, "Everybody Loves Somebody", knocking the Beatles from No 1 position in 1964. For the next 20 years or so, Dean was one of the top draws in Las Vegas and elsewhere. His television appearances perpetuated the public's opinion of him as a laid-back half-drunk crooner, who was also a ladies man. His persona as a drinker was reflected in his car license plate, DRUNKY, although it has been said that he often drank only apple juice during his television shows.

His membership of the Rat Pack with Sinatra, Peter Lawford, Sammy Davis, Jr, *et al*, added to his wild-living reputation and, although he participated fully in the boozy alliance, was often first to leave the party, particularly when film or television work was on the next day's schedule. In 1965, he starred in his own NBC networked TV series, *The Dean Martin Show*, which ran for nine seasons. Many more television specials, as well as the 'Matt Helm' series of films followed this. By the late 1970s, health problems restricted Dean to the casino show stages. In 1987, his son Dean Paul Martin, a fighter pilot in the California Air National Guard, was killed in a crash; devastated by the loss, Dean never got over it, and became even more withdrawn and virtually reclusive.

Dean Martin died of respiratory failure on Christmas Day 1995. Las Vegas dimmed the lights on the Strip in homage, and named a road, Dean Martin Drive, in his memory.

AL MARTINO

Birth name: Jasper Cini
Born: October 7, 1927, Philadelphia, Pennsylvania
Died: October 13, 2009, Springfield, Pennsylvania
Years active: 1948 - 2009
Record label(s): Capitol

A l Martino had his greatest success as a singer between the early 1950s and mid-1970s as one of the great Italian American pop crooners but he is equally remembered for his role as swarthy singer Johnny Fontane in The Godfather.

Jasper "Al" Cini was born in Philadelphia, Pennsylvania, on October 7, 1927. The name Jasper was an Anglicisation of his father's name, Gasparino. His parents were immigrants from Abruzzo, Italy, who ran a construction business, and while growing up he worked alongside his brothers as a bricklayer. He was inspired to become a singer by emulating artists such as Al Jolson and Perry Como, and by the success of a family friend, Alfredo Cocozza, who had changed his name to Mario Lanza.

After serving with the US Navy in World War II, during which he was wounded in the Iwo Jima invasion, Cini began his singing career. Encouraged by Lanza, he adopted the stage name Al Martino and began singing in local nightclubs. In 1948 he moved to New York, recorded some songs for the Jubilee label and in 1952 won first place on Arthur Godfrey's Talent Scouts' television programme with a performance of Perry Como's hit "If".

As a result, he won a recording contract with the Philadelphia-based independent label BBS, where he recorded the song "Here in My Heart". Lanza had been asked by his label RCA Victor to record the song, but Al called and pleaded with him not to do so in order to let his version have a clear run. The song spent three weeks at No. 1 on the US pop charts in June 1952, earning Al a gold disc and, later in the year, also reached the top of the UK charts. It was No. 1 in the first UK Singles Chart, published by the New Musical Express on November 14, 1952, earning him a place in the Guinness Book of World Records. "Here in My Heart" remained in the top position for nine weeks in the UK, a record for the longest consecutive run at No. 1 that has only since been beaten by five other songs.

The record's success led to a deal with Capitol Records, and he released three more singles — "Take My Heart," "Rachel," and "When You're Mine" — through 1953, all of which hit the US Top 40. However, his success also attracted the attention of the Mafia, who bought out Al's management contract and ordered him to pay $75,000 as a safeguard for their investment. After making a down-payment to appease them, he moved to Britain. His popularity allowed him to continue to perform and record successfully in the UK, headlining at the London Palladium and having six further British chart hits in the period up to 1955, including "Now" and "Wanted". However, his work received

LITTLE BOOK OF CROONERS

no exposure back in the US. In 1958, thanks to the help of an influential family friend, Al returned to the US and resumed his recording career but he faced difficulties in re-establishing himself especially with the arrival of rock and roll.

His perseverance paid off and in 1963, he had his biggest US chart success with "I Love You Because", a cover of Leon Payne's 1950 country music classic. Al had four other US top 10 hits in 1963 and 1964 - "Painted, Tainted Rose" (1963), "I Love You More and More Every Day", "Tears and Roses" and "Silver Bells" (all 1964). One of his biggest hits was "Spanish Eyes", achieving several gold and platinum discs for sales. Recorded in 1965, the song reached No. 5 on the UK Singles Chart when re-issued in 1973 and still remains amongst the 50 most played songs worldwide.

Al was a natural to play the role of Johnny Fontane in the 1972 film The Godfather, as well as singing the film's theme, "Speak Softly Love". He played the same role in The Godfather Part III and was also somewhat typecast as the ageing crooner Sal Stevens in the short film Cut Out, in 2006.

Al died on October 13, 2009 at his childhood home in Springfield, Pennsylvania, six days after his 82nd birthday. He was buried at Holy Cross Cemetery in Culver City, California, and was survived by his wife, Judi, son Alfred and daughter Allison

JOHNNY MATHIS

Birth name: John Royce Mathis
Born: September 30 1935, Gilmer, Texas
Years active: 1956 – present
Record label(s): Columbia (now Sony), Mercury

E merging into the music industry in the latter end of the 50s, Johnny Mathis was one of the last of the traditional male singers to emerge before the rock era began. With a series of popular records Mathis became the USA's third best-selling male singer, after Elvis Presley and Frank Sinatra, with over 350 million records sold. Over 60 of his albums made the Billboard charts, with over a third of these achieving the coveted gold or platinum status. He was also the first black entertainer to become a millionaire before the age of 21.

Johnny Mathis was born in Gilmer, Texas, on September 30 1935, the fourth of seven children. His parents, Clem and Mildred Mathis moved to San Francisco, California, while Johnny was young, and raised their family there. At an early age his father, a former vaudeville performer, spotted his son's talent and bought an old piano for $25, to encourage him to develop his musical education. He also taught Johnny some song and dance routines that entertained visitors to their home, eventually leading to public performances at school concerts and at church events. When Mathis was 13, his father enrolled him with a voice teacher, Connie Cox, who agreed to the arrangement that her pupil would pay for lessons by doing odd jobs around her house. For six years he studied under Connie's guidance, improving his voice projection, practising vocal scales, and learning classical operatic techniques.

At high school, Johnny became a star athlete in track and field as a hurdler and notably, a high jumper, as well as being a very competent basketball player. This led to a scholarship at San Francisco State College to study for teaching qualifications in English and Physical Education. He broke the college high jump record in 1954, with a leap of 6ft 5in. While performing at a college function, he was spotted by Helen Noga, the owner of The Black Hawk Club, who became his manager. At a weekend singing performance, his manager had brought George Avakian, a producer from Columbia Records, to hear him. Impressed by Mathis, he sent a well-documented telegram to the Columbia bosses, "Have found phenomenal 19-year-old who could go all the way. Send blank contracts." This they did, and before long, Avakian's prophecy was fulfilled.

One other major honour to come the way of Mathis was an invitation to attend for trials for the 1956 USA Olympic athletics team. Advised by his father, he travelled instead to New York to make his first recordings that were released in 1956. His first album, *Johnny Mathis: A New Sound in Popular Song*, was jazz-orientated and a slow seller. His

LITTLE BOOK OF CROONERS

producer at Columbia, the famous Mitch Miller, steered Mathis away from jazz towards the soft, romantic ballads that were to become his hallmark. Two of his 1956 recordings, "Wonderful, Wonderful", and "It's Not For Me To Say", the latter used on the soundtrack of the film *Lizzie* in the following year, soon became classics of the genre. After appearing on the *Ed Sullivan Show,* and small parts in a couple of movies, his future stardom was assured. Mathis bought himself a mansion in the Hollywood Hills district, formerly the residence of Howard Hughes; he still lives there today. He then set up his own companies Jon Mat Records Inc, which handled his recording interests, and Rojon Productions Inc, to look after all his concert and personal appearance business. Since the death of his business manager in 1984, Johnny has managed all aspects of his own career from his offices in Burbank, California.

Apart from a three-year period in the 1960s, Mathis has remained with Columbia/Sony for his entire recording career in which he made over 350 million record sales spanning a wide variety of musical styles including jazz, Latin-American, soul, R&B and country, as well his Christmas songs. His 110 albums and over 200 singles are testament to his popularity and longevity as a recording star. His album *Johnny's Greatest Hits* stayed in the *Billboard* Album Charts for 490 consecutive weeks, or 9½ years, the *Guinness Book of Records* confirming a feat unmatched by any other performer. Only two others, Frank Sinatra and Barry Manilow have equalled his achievement of having five albums in the *Billboard* charts, simultaneously. His career, spanning six decades, has brought Mathis three *Grammy* awards and six nominations, and two Oscar nominations for soundtrack songs. He has made 12 television specials and appeared on over 300 other TV shows.

2013 was a milestone year for Mathis. Having achieved his 50th Billboard Adult Contemporary Chart hit, he has appeared on various Billboard charts for seven decades in a row! He has scaled down his workload but still continues to perform live and played at major venues on both sides of the Atlantic in 2014 headlining in London, Birmingham and Manchester in April of that year.

LEFT
Johnny Mathis in 1968.

BELOW
Johnny Mathis singing in the 1970s.

LITTLE BOOK OF CROONERS

MATT
MONRO

Birth name: Terence Edward Parsons
Born: December 1 1930, Shoreditch, London
Died: February 7 1985, Cromwell Hospital, London
Years active: Mid 1950s – 1984
Record label(s): Decca, Fontana, Parlophone, Capitol, Columbia

Known as 'The Singer's Singer', many of his contemporaries admired the artistry of the man, even though they were rivals in the same business. Great stars paid compliments to his singing, one paid tribute after his death with these words, "His pitch was right on the nose: his word enunciations letter perfect: his understanding of a song thorough. He will be missed very much not only by me, but by his fans all over the world". So said the great Frank Sinatra: he was speaking about Matt Monro.

Terence Edward Parsons was born in Shoreditch, London, on December 1 1930, the youngest of five children. His father died when he was only three and, when his mother became ill, Terence moved to live with a foster family. Leaving school at the age of 14, he did a series of menial jobs before entering the British army at the age of 17½ years. Two years later he volunteered for overseas duty, and was posted to Hong Kong as a tank driving instructor. Having previously sung at his local dance hall in North London, he continued to sing during his army service in the Far East. There, he entered many talent competitions and became such a frequent winner that he was barred from entering again. In compensation, he was given his own radio show, *Terry Parsons Sings*.

On leaving the army in 1953, he became a bus driver in London. After his day job, Terence sang with dance bands, using the names Terry Fitzgerald and Al Jordan. He also made demo records of new songs for music publishers in Denmark Street, London. A record of "Polka Dots and Moonbeams" that he had made on an earlier trip to Glasgow was heard by the famous pianist Winifred Atwell and was passed by her to Decca, who auditioned Terence, then promptly gave him a recording contract. His name was changed to Matt Monro around that time. As well as appearing on Radio Luxembourg, he also sang with the BBC Show Band, and on Winifred Atwell's television show. Commercial jingles featured prominently in Matt's life; he recorded over 40 for radio and TV advertisements in 12 years.

George Martin, the famous EMI producer, asked Matt to record a demo in the style of Sinatra, to be used as a guide for Peter Sellers to copy, for his next album, *Songs For Swinging Sellers* (1959). A change of plan saw it included, unchanged, on the album with the singer being credited as 'Fred Flange'. Martin then signed Matt to the Parlophone label, a move that soon produced Matt's major hit, "Portrait Of My Love" in 1960. The next six years saw the label issue Matt's 19 singles, eight EPs and four albums. Hits such as "My Kind Of Girl", "From Russia With Love", "Softly As I Leave You", "Born Free" and the

LITTLE BOOK OF CROONERS

atmospheric, "Walk Away" enhanced Monro's reputation internationally, and led to him signing for Capitol in the US, when the label sought a big name after the death of Nat King Cole in 1965.

Matt moved to America where he appeared at major venues, including several Las Vegas casinos, and on many top television shows. His following in Latin America led to him recording the first of many albums in Spanish, one of which went platinum, Matt's first. On returning to the UK, Matt was signed by Columbia and made more hit records, alongside his TV appearances, cabaret tours and theatre shows.

Few at the time new that Matt was an alcoholic. Despite the efforts of his manager Don Black, the addiction continued, as did his heavy smoking. On stage, Matt was the consummate professional, his performances giving no indication of his predilection for strong drink, although it began to affect his health. His last single, "And You Smiled" (1973) entered the Top 30. A 1980 compilation album *Heartbreakers* went gold within a few days after release. By this time Matt was becoming very ill, his liver ravaged by alcohol; he was persuaded that a transplant was the only option. During the surgical operation it was discovered that he had cancer, which had reached an advanced stage, so the transplant was abandoned.

Matt discharged himself from hospital and resumed his stage performances. His recording career was over but he wanted to continue singing for his fans while he was able. His final performance took place in the Barbican Centre, London. The sell-out audience and media critics alike were impressed by the performance that ended with an emotional Matt receiving a poignant, seven-minute standing ovation.

Matt Monro died at the age of 54, in the Cromwell Hospital, London, on February 7 1985. Arguably, Britain's finest ballad singer, the man who was many times voted Britain's No 1 vocalist, was gone. His voice lives on in his legacy of many wonderful recordings.

JOHNNIE
RAY

Birth name: John Alvin Ray
Born: January 10, 1927, Hopewell, Oregon, US
Died: February 24, 1990, Los Angeles, US
Years active: 1951 - 1989
Record label(s): Okeh Records, Columbia Records

Although Johnnie Ray is rightly revered as a crooner he is credited as a major precursor of what would become rock and roll with his animated stage personality influencing a new generation of performers.

The publication, British Hit Singles & Albums, observed that Johnnie was "a sensation in the 1950s, the heart-wrenching vocal delivery of the 'Cry Guy' ... influenced many acts including Elvis and was the prime target for teen hysteria in the pre-Presley days."

In the US, he quickly rose from obscurity to stardom in 1952 and also became a major star in the UK by the following year. But his star only shone brightly for a few years and by the end of the decade his career began to decline and his American record label dropped him in 1960.

He never regained a strong following and very rarely appeared on American television after 1973. His fan base in other countries, however, remained strong until his last year of performing, in 1989, and his recordings never stopped selling outside of the US.

Born in January 1927, his musical achievements were all the more meritorious as he was totally deaf in one ear after a trampoline accident when he was 13 and he performed wearing a hearing aid. Surgery in New York in 1958 left him almost completely deaf in both ears.

Inspired by rhythm singers such as Kay Starr, LaVern Baker and Ivory Joe Hunter, Johnnie developed a unique rhythm-based style, described as alternating between pre-rock R&B and a more conventional classic pop approach.

His first record, the self-penned R&B number, "Whiskey and Gin," was a minor hit in 1951 and the following year he dominated the charts with the double-sided hit single of "Cry" and "The Little White Cloud That Cried". Selling over two million copies of the 78rpm single, Ray's sexually-charged delivery struck a chord with teenagers and he quickly became a teen idol.

The Hollywood studio 20th Century Fox capitalized on his superstardom by including him in the ensemble cast of the movie There's No Business Like Show Business (1954) alongside Ethel Merman as his mother, Dan Dailey as his father, Donald O'Connor as his brother and Marilyn Monroe as his sister-in-law.

Johnnie's performing style was pure theatrics later associated with rock and roll icons such as Elvis Presley, including tearing at his hair, falling to the floor, and crying. He quickly earned the nicknames "Mr. Emotion", "The Nabob of Sob", and "The Prince of Wails".

LITTLE BOOK OF CROONERS

More hits followed in the mid-1950s, including "Please Mr. Sun," "Such a Night," "Walkin' My Baby Back Home," "A Sinner Am I" and "Yes Tonight Josephine." He had a UK number one with "Just Walkin' in the Rain" (which he initially hated) during the Christmas season in 1956.

Though his American popularity was declining in the late 1950s, he remained popular in the UK breaking the box-office record at the London Palladium formerly set by Frankie Laine.

Asked about his appeal to his mostly female audience, Johnnie replied: " I've got no talent. Still sing flat as a table. I'm a sort of human spaniel. People come to see what I'm like. I make them feel, I exhaust them, I destroy them. "

Although he was married and had relationships with women, Johnnie was arrested twice for soliciting men for sex. He was rumoured to also have had a long-term relationship with his manager Bill Franklin.

He had a sympathetic ally in Judy Garland, performing as her opening act during her last concerts in Copenhagen, Denmark and Malmo, Sweden. Johnnie was also the best man during Garland's wedding to nightclub manager Mickey Deans in London in 1969.

Johnnie drank regularly throughout his life and had been hospitalized for tuberculosis in 1960. He recovered but continued drinking and was diagnosed with cirrhosis at the age of 50. On February 24, 1990, Johnnie died of liver failure at Cedars-Sinai Hospital in Los Angeles.

As Dexy's Midnight Runners stated in their 1982 hit "Come On Eileen" … Poor old Johnnie Ray sounded sad upon the radio / He moved a million hearts in mono.

JIM
REEVES

Birth name: James Travis Reeves
Born: August 20, 1923, Galloway, Texas, US
Died: July 31, 1964, Davidson County, Tennesee, US
Years active: 1949 - 1964
Record label(s): RCA Victor, Fabor, Macy, Abbott

Gentleman Jim Reeves was one of the best of the 'Nashville-Sound' country and western crooners. Born in 1923, in Panola County, Texas, after graduating from college he began to pursue a professional baseball career but was sidelined by an injury to his leg while a pitcher with Houston Buffaloes.

Jim began to work as a radio announcer, and sang live between songs. During the late 1940s, he was contracted with a couple of small Texas-based recording companies but without success. Influenced by such Western swing-music artists as Jimmie Rodgers and Moon Mullican, as well as popular singers Bing Crosby, Eddy Arnold and Frank Sinatra, he made some early swing recordings such as "Each Beat of my Heart" and "My Heart's Like a Welcome Mat" from the late 1940s to the early 1950s.

Jim's' first successful country music songs included "I Love You" (a duet with Ginny Wright), "Mexican Joe", and "Bimbo" which reached Number 1 in 1954 on the US Country Charts. In 1955, he was signed to a 10-year recording contract with RCA Victor by Steve Sholes, who signed Elvis Presley for the company that same year. Also in 1955, he joined the Grand Ole Opry and made his first appearance on ABC-TV's Ozark Jubilee, where he was a fill-in host from May to July in 1958.

For his earliest RCA recordings, Jim was still singing with the loud style of his first recordings, considered standard for country and western performers at that time. He decided to decrease his volume, using a lower pitch and singing with lips nearly touching the microphone, although RCA was not particularly supportive. During 1957, with the endorsement of his producer Chet Atkins, he used this style for his version of a demonstration song of lost love intended for a female singer. "Four Walls" not only scored No. 1 on the country music charts but reached No. 11 on the national charts. Jim had helped launch a new style of country music, using violins and lusher background arrangements that was soon known as the Nashville sound.

Jim became known as a crooner because of his rich light baritone voice. Songs such as "Adios Amigo", "Welcome to My World", and "Am I Losing You?" perfectly demonstrated this. His Christmas songs were also perennial favourites, including "C-H-R-I-S-T-M-A-S", "Blue Christmas" and "An Old Christmas Card".

The peak of his career came in 1959 with the success of the Joe Allison composition "He'll Have to Go", which reached number 2 in the US charts and number 12 in Britain, ultimately selling three million copies. Country music historian Bill Malone lauded Jim's

LITTLE BOOK OF CROONERS

vocal styling referring to him as "the singer with the velvet touch."

After his success he made successful tours of the US, Scandinavia and South Africa, where he starred in a film, Kimberley Jim (1963) and recorded songs in the local Afrikaans language.

Jim had been planning more tours and television appearances at the time his Beechcraft Debonair aircraft went down in bad weather on July 31, 1964, in Hendersonville, Tennessee, near Nashville - taking the lives of Jim and his business manager.

Jim's widow, Mary, released many of his back-catalogue recordings after his death to great success - so much so that younger executives in the record business had to be reminded that Jim has been gone for over 35 years!

He even had an album reach Gold status in Denmark in 1999! It is a source of great frustration to Jim's fans and family that his great repertoire of music does not get equal airplay today in the US compared with other deceased artists such as Patsy Cline.

But Jim's legacy still lives on, as one of the greatest voices in recorded music, country or otherwise. Let Jim have the last word on his popularity: "Maybe it's just that I sound as if I enjoy what I'm doing. I don't work too hard at it. I never press. I just go on doing what I enjoy doing, and if other people like it I'm glad. After all, this is the only life we get. We just come through here once and I believe in making it a satisfying experience."

LEFT & BELOW
Jim Reeves

FRANK
SINATRA

Birth name: Francis Albert Sinatra
Born: December 12 1915, Paterson Hospital, New Jersey
Died: May 14 1998, Los Angeles, California
Years active: 1930s – 1990s
Record label(s): Columbia, RCA Victor, Capitol, Reprise

Threading that influenced me most was the way Tommy (Dorsey) played his trombone. It was my idea to make my voice work in the same way as a trombone or violin – not sounding like them, but 'playing' the voice like those instrumentalists." – Frank Sinatra. The man known as 'The Chairman of The Board', also said, "Throughout my career, if I have done anything, I have paid attention to every note and every word I sing - if I respect the song. If I cannot project this to a listener, I fail."

Francis Albert Sinatra, the man who sold over 250 million records and became one of the most influential entertainment figures in the twentieth century, was born in a Paterson, New Jersey, hospital. His parents were both immigrant Italians, father Anthony Sinatra was a boiler-man and his mother Natalie 'Dolly' Garaventa Sinatra, a midwife and part-time Democratic Party ward organiser. Frank was brought up in a relatively comfortable middle class family in Hoboken, New Jersey. In 1935, he was in a group called the Hoboken Four that won a local talent show, the prize being a tour with the promoter. After working as a waiter and singing at clubs, Frank was heard on the radio by bandleader Harry James, who hired him; they made their first record together in July 1939. By the end of that year, Frank had joined Tommy Dorsey and, in 1940, reached No 1 on the Billboard charts with "I'll Never Smile Again". Unfit for military service due to a damaged eardrum at birth, the Sinatra career, both on records with Columbia, and on radio, progressed as a solo artist with Frank making many great recordings.

By the late 1940s, Sinatra had lost favour with his mainly teenage fans, and also damaged his image in a series of public altercations, particularly one in which he punched a journalist. After some lean years, Sinatra began to make a big impact as a movie actor, notably in *From Here To Eternity* (1953), winning Best Supporting Actor at the Academy Awards, and in *The Man With The Golden Arm* (1955) that saw him nominated for Best Actor.

He switched labels to Capitol in 1953, resulting in notable successes with the more upbeat albums such as *Songs For Swinging Lovers*, and hit singles that dominated the charts for four years. Networked television shows and cinema films helped his annual income rise to $4 million. The 1960 founding of his own Reprise label during the Rat Pack years, and a friendship with President John F Kennedy that brought allegations of Mafia involvement in JFK's primary elections, kept the often controversial Sinatra in the public domain. Several of his family members had connections with some high-profile gangsters;

LITTLE BOOK OF CROONERS

this led to JFK distancing his presidency from Frank, who later supported the Republican campaign of Nixon.

By 1970, Frank was contemplating retirement but made several 'comeback' appearances on the road, often playing to larger audiences than had frequented the Las Vegas casinos he had played in for many years. In the 1980 presidential elections he threw his support, plus around $4 million, behind the Reagan campaign, later calling in the favour of the elected Reagan as a character reference, to offset the allegations of Sinatra's Mafia connections, in Sinatra's application for a Nevada casino licence.

The same year found Frank releasing his first album for six years, *Trilogy: Past Present Future.* Controversy came with Frank's $2 million contract to sing at Sun City, South Africa, during apartheid, in 1981. This was curiously at odds with his stance against segregation in the US, where he was a leader, together with Sammy Davis, Jr, in the fight to break down racial intolerance in clubs and at casino venues.

Honours came thick and fast for Frank: the Kennedy Center Honor in 1983, the Presidential Medal of Freedom in 1965, and an Honorary Doctor of Engineering degree, which met with protests from students, at his home town Institute of Technology. Frank kept working up to the early 1990s; his two *Duets* albums sold millions of copies. A richly deserved *Grammy* Lifetime Achievement Award complemented a career total of 10 Grammys in 1994.

LEFT
Frank Sinatra on tour in 1976.

BELOW
Frank Sinatra in a promotional portrait for one of his many films.

Sinatra was married four times, to Nancy Barbato, Ava Gardner, Mia Farrow and Barbara Marx, and had other romantic attachments including Lauren Bacall. He had three children, Nancy, Frank, Jr and Christina, all of whom he adored. By his early 80s, most of Frank's friends had passed on; the loss of his friend Dean Martin hit him hard. After suffering a stroke and two heart attacks, Frank Sinatra passed away on May 14 1998. He was buried close to his Rancho Mirage property, near Palm Springs, allegedly wearing a blue suit, and with a bottle of Jack Daniels, a pack of Camel cigarettes, and a Zippo lighter. Ol' Blue Eyes finally did it 'His' Way.

RUDY
VALLEE

Birth name: Hubert Prior Vallee
Born: July 28 1901, Island Pond, Vermont
Died: July 3 1986, Hollywood, California
Years active: 1920s – 1970s
Record label(s): Velvet Tone Records (1928-33), Viva, ABM*, Pearl Flapper*, RKO Unique Records*
(*recent re-releases)

A man with a reputation for being arrogant, egotistical and hot tempered would seem an unlikely candidate to become a popular music and film idol. He was reputed to have been very difficult to work for and was occasionally stricken with stage fright. At times, after he had abandoned his trade mark megaphone for the electric microphone, he was known to have turned his back on his audience and sang facing the band. His temper got the better of him on several occasions when he left the stage to punch a member of the audience who had failed to appreciate his greatness and had heckled him.

Some music historians claim that Vallee, not Gene Austin, was the first of the 'crooners'. He could well have been so, although his continued use of the megaphone after the general adoption of the microphone may have led some to form an incorrect conclusion. His recording career was much less prolific than that of Austin, but he was a major performer on radio, in theatres and later, in the movies, a heartthrob who made the flappers of the day swoon wherever he appeared. Rudy Vallee was born Hubert Prior Vallee on July 28 1901, in Island Pond, Vermont, and grew up in Westbrook, Maine. Vallee adopted the nickname Rudy after his idol, saxophonist Rudy Weidtoft. He took up the saxophone and clarinet while at high school, and also learned to play the drums: these musical skills were put to use in his youth, playing with bands around the New England area.

In 1917, Rudy volunteered for the US Navy but was discharged when they discovered he was underage. He found a job as a movie projectionist before entering the University of Maine in 1921. The following autumn, he transferred to Yale University, studying languages and philosophy, paying his fees and living expenses by playing in country clubs and at dances. He joined the Yale Collegians band and began to sing, using a megaphone to enhance his voice. Vallee dropped out of Yale in 1924 and went to London for a year, where he played saxophone with the Savoy Hotel band.

After returning to Yale, he took his degree in philosophy, and played in the college marching band. After graduation, Rudy went first to Boston and then New York, where he joined an orchestra. He later met Bert Lown, a bandleader, who set up a group fronted by Vallee, which made its debut at the Heigh-Ho Club in January 1928. This band consisted of two violins, two saxophones and a piano; they played only choruses, with Vallee singing songs in several Latin languages through his megaphone.

Radio dates soon followed and Vallee's fame and fortune began to grow, along with his ego: a one-year long theatre tour for Paramount earned him $12,500, a considerable

LITTLE BOOK OF CROONERS

income in the time of the Great Depression. His popularity soared, leading to his first film in 1929, *The Vagabond Love,* and his own radio series, as host, on *The Fleischmann's Yeast Musical Variety Hour.* Radio engagements lasted well into the 1940s. With his band, The Connecticut Yankees, he made recordings of "The Stein Song", a University song from Maine, and "Vieni, Vieni" toward the end of the 1930s. The band also made numerous live performances in which Rudy continued to delight his largely female audiences; his good looks and light tenor voice, which developed into a baritone in later years, made him the most sought after singer in the US for many years.

Film work continued, the 1942 comedy *The Palm Beach Story* being acclaimed as one of his best, along with another comedy role in the 1955 release *Gentlemen Marry Brunettes*. The 1943 recording of "As Time Goes By", his last major hit, was made while he performed with the Coast Guard Band, entertaining US troops. Further acting success on the Broadway stage, in shows like *How To Succeed In Business Without Really Trying* was rewarded with a role in the film version. In the 60s, Rudy appeared in the Batman television series, and made guest appearances on celebrity shows, while his work in films continued until the 1970s.

Rumoured to have been bisexual, he was married four times; his second wife was the young actress Jane Greer. Rudy also had a much-publicised affair with actress Hedy Lamarr and, as his ego led him to disclose, at least 144 other starlets. He married his last wife, Eleanor Norris, in 1946; this marriage endured until Vallee's death in 1986. Eleanor later wrote her memoirs entitled *My Vagabond Lover* in which she gives a biographical insight into the life of one of the most famous American entertainers of all time.

Rudy Vallee died at the age of 84 while watching a television show. His fame was such that his headstone was stolen from the cemetery at Westbrook in Maine.

SCOTT
WALKER

Birth name: Noel Scott Engel
Born: January 9 1943
Years active: 1958 – present
Record label(s): Tower, Universal, Philips, Columbia, Virgin, Fontana, Mercury, 4AD

Scott Walker is a musical enigma. First, a solo artist and teen idol, and later becoming a member of a group that achieved massive popularity by singing melodic popular ballads. Then, a solo career that saw him gradually shift away from the popular songs that had made him an international star, as part of The Walker Brothers, into a more soulful and self-indulgent style that encompassed the works of Jacques Brel. His albums of mostly self-written songs with thought-provoking lyrics and a darker musical feel alienated him from his original fan base. Walker has admitted complacency in his choice of material, and the over-reliance on slow tempo in his albums.

Noel Scott Engel was born on January 9 1943 in Hamilton, Ohio, but grew up in New York. Scott's childhood ambition was to become an actor, although music was to become the new direction in his life. He became an accomplished bass guitar player and also recorded under the name Scotty Engel. After moving to Hollywood, he worked as a session bassist before joining a band called The Routers. It was not long before Scott teamed up with another singer, John Maus, and the duo appeared as The Dalton Brothers; they were soon joined by drummer Gary Leeds and the trio became The Walker Brothers.

After crossing the Atlantic in 1965, the group regularly made it to the top of the British charts over the next two years. A rich baritone voice and a stylish, but enigmatic stage persona helped Scott to become popular; his somewhat reclusive choice of lifestyle did not endear him to his manager, Maurice King, who wanted him to exploit his popularity. The Walker Brothers split up in 1967 when Scott, the principal songwriter, grew tired of the concept and had started writing songs for his own future solo performance. The Scott Walker phenomenon seemed almost unstoppable: his first four albums reached the UK Top 10; the second album reached the coveted No 1 position in the 1968 charts. His recordings included a mixture of self-composed material, middle of the road standards, and the more avant garde works of the Belgian composer, Jacques Brel. One of his Brel songs, "Jackie", contained the words "…authentic queers" and other 'unsuitable' references, and was promptly banned by the, then, almost puritanical BBC, thus reducing its exposure to the record buying public of the day.

His fourth album, *Scott 4*, was notable in that it contained only songs written by the performer: its impact was devalued by the almost simultaneous release, by the BBC, of the album *Scott Sings Songs From His Television Series*. Sales of his solo album were adversely affected, and Scott became more downbeat about the progress and direction of his career.

LITTLE BOOK OF CROONERS

In 1970, Walker released one of his more critically acclaimed albums, *'Til The Band Comes In,* which stood the test of time and was re-released in 1996. The 1972 album, *The Moviegoer,* consisted entirely of film themes and soundtrack songs, including "Speak Softly Love" from *The Godfather.* His 1973 album *Stretch* was a collection of country songs followed by *We Had It All* a year later. A brief resurrection of The Walker Brothers, in 1975, spawned three albums that were moderately successful: the first single release, "No Regrets" rose to the No 7 position in the UK charts.

After the Walker Brothers last album in 1978, six years elapsed before Scott released the 1984 solo album *Climate of Hunter.* This recording reflected the contemporary music style and, curiously, four of its tracks bore only the track number as their title, "Track Three" being an example: this album was re-released in January 2006. Another decade passed before Walker's next offering, *Tilt* in 1995, in which Scott recorded his vocals once only for each track, with no retakes, over the previously recorded musical backing that included the Sinfonia Strings of London, and a church pipe organ.

The soundtrack album *Pola X,* from the eponymous French film, emerged in 1999, which Scott wrote and also produced. With further soundtrack credits in *To Have And To Hold* and the James Bond film *The World Is Not Enough,* in which he sang "Only Myself To Blame", the career of Scott Walker began to move onward. Around the turn of the millennium he became influential in the career of the pop group Pulp, and produced their album *We Love Life* that was released in 2001. Honoured in 2003 for his contribution to music by the magazine *Q,* only the third to receive such an award, Walker received a standing ovation at the presentation ceremony.

4AD Records released Scott's first album for 11 years in 2006, entitled Drift, to critical acclaim and it remained in the album charts for several months. His last album for the label was Bish Bosch in 2012 and more recently as a record producer or guest performer he has worked with a number of contemporary artists including Pulp and Bat For Lashes.

ANDY
WILLIAMS

Birth name: Howard Andrew Williams
Born: December 3 1927, Wall Lake, Iowa
Died: September 25, 2012 Branson, Missouri, US
Years active: Late 1930s – present
Record label(s): RCA Victor X, Cadence Records, Columbia, Varese

A ndy Williams first sang in public at the age of eight, in a quartet with his three older brothers, and was still singing some 70 years later with regular appearances in his own theatre, The Andy Williams Moon River Theatre, in Branson, Missouri, which he built in 1992. A modest and self-effacing man who, in a career that earned him 18 gold album awards and three platinum records, once said, "I still don't think I'm as good as anyone else."

Howard Andrew Williams was born on December 3 1927 in Wall Lake, Iowa, youngest of four boys. The Williams Brothers Quartet sang with the local church choir, and soon became established favourites on local radio in nearby Des Moines, and later in Chicago and Cincinatti, where Andy attended high school. The quartet was spotted by Bing Crosby, who included the boys on his 1944 hit single, "Swinging On A Star". Their fame spread with appearances in two 1944 films, Janie and Kansas City Kitty, and two more musical films in 1947, Something In The Wind and Ladies' Man. Work on the cabaret circuit, with singer Kay Thompson in 1947, continued until the quartet dissolved their act in 1951, when Andy decided to seek his solo singing fortune in New York.

A recording contract in 1952, with RCA Victor's X label, yielded six singles that failed to trouble the charts. Andy was given a regular spot on Steve Allen's Tonight television show in 1955, the year he was also signed to the small, New York based, Cadence Records label. This contract was the catalyst to Andy's recording success: the third release in 1956, "Canadian Sunset," entered the Top 10 followed by his only Billboard No1 hit, "Butterfly", and another Top 10 hit, "I Like Your Kind of Love." Further chart entries were achieved with "The Hawaiian Wedding Song," "Are You Sincere," "The Village of St Bernadette," and "Lonely Street," before Andy moved to Los Angeles in 1961, to sign for Columbia.

The Columbia contract was the biggest recording contract ever awarded to a solo artist up until that time. Andy's albums could hardly fail to hit the charts: "Moon River" and "Days Of Wine and Roses", the second of which reached No 1 in 1963, and stayed there for 16 weeks, were testimony to his popularity. Many more of his albums reached the charts in the 1960s and early 70s, earning 17 of his gold discs by 1973. Andy was also asked to sing at three Oscar ceremonies in 1962, when he sang "Moon River," and again in 1966 and 1967, on each occasion performing songs by Henry Mancini.

LITTLE BOOK OF CROONERS

Although considered to be primarily an album artist, Andy also hit the singles charts with such unforgettable songs as "Can't Get Used to Losing You," "Happy Heart," and, in 1970, the theme from the film Love Story, "Where Do I Begin." Andy also made a total of eight Christmas albums.

On television, Andy's guest appearances on the Tonight shows led to an almost inevitable series of his own in 1962, The Andy Williams Show, which won three Emmy Awards for the best variety show. The series ran for almost 10 years before Andy decided to quit at the top of his popularity, and limited his television appearances to three 'specials' per year. He also made a large number of concert tours over the years. Apart from a series of half-hour shows in 1976-77, he kept to the three shows a year format on an occasional basis until the 1990s, before giving up touring and regular television appearances to devote his energies to opening his own theatre in Branson, Missouri.

Far from slowing down his schedule, Andy continued to appear in as many as 12 shows a week in his theatre each autumn, and made the occasional European tour. In 2002, Andy recorded a duet version of his hit, "Can't Take My Eyes Off You," with the British singer, Denise Van Outen.

Andy was twice married, first to singer and ex-Folies Bergère dancer, Claudine Longet, in 1961 with whom he had three children. After their divorce in 1975, Andy supported his ex-wife when she was charged with the 1976 murder of her partner, the ski-star Vladmir Sabich, and shielded their children from the publicity surrounding the event. His second, and enduring marriage, to Debbie Haas, took place in 1991 and they lived together in Branson, Missouri. In a surprise appearance at his home-town theatre in November 2011, Andy confirmed that he had been diagnosed with bladder cancer and barely a year later he died at the age of 84.

**The pictures in this book were
provided courtesy of the following:**

GETTY IMAGES
101 Bayham Street, London NW1 0AG

Design & Artwork: SCOTT GIARNESE

Published by: DEMAND MEDIA LIMITED & G2 ENTERTAINMENT LIMITED

Publishers: JASON FENWICK & JULES GAMMOND